BROWSING IN THE MORGUE

The Best from Montana's Early Newspapers

Compiled by Russell B. Hill

Barlow Press   Helena, Montana

Cover background: Montana's 315 general-circulation English-language newspapers published before 1900.

Barlow Press
P.O. Box 5403
Helena, Montana 59604

Printed in the United States of America.

First edition
92 91 90 89 88   5 4 3 2 1

Library of Congress Catalog Card Number: 86-072926
ISBN 0-940755-00-9

To Montana's journalists,
dead and alive,
for raking leaves in the wind.

CHEAPER THAN EVER.

LOW

PRICES

WILL

TELL!

We

Are Now

RECEIVING

Our

Immense

Stock of

FALL & WINTER CLOTHING

FOR MEN AND BOYS.

Which we Offer Now at the Lowest

CASH STATES PRICES
At Wholesale and Retail.

Our Stock Comprises
Everything for Men's Wear,
Which will be Sold at PANIC PRICES

HOLZMAN & BRO.

The Helena Independent, September 27, 1876

PREFACE

Morgue is the term cynically applied by journalists to the in-house libraries of newspapers and magazines, files of clippings where articles are buried as soon as they are printed, theoretically preserved for future reference but essentially consigned to oblivion.

Browsing in the Morgue resurrects 55 Montana newspaper articles published between 1867 and 1899. The articles were selected from among 315 general-circulation English-language newspapers printed in the state before the turn of the century, newspapers with names like the *Sheridan Paper, Stinking Water Prospector, Montana Radiator, Montana Vociferator, Keep Off the Grass, Big Hole Breezes, Our Visitor,* and even a handwritten *Big Elk Budget.*

Only locally written articles are included here, and they are printed in their entirety, with most spelling and punctuation errors preserved. Wire service stories and exchanges from other newspapers were excluded, despite the tempting addition of locally written headlines: "The Brainless Fools," for instance, or "William Stone Murdered Everybody."

Many good friends contributed to this collection. Michael Crater, Tom Palmer, and of course my wife, Jan, generously offered their suggestions, corrections, and encouragement. Jeanette Barnes Geary, who designed the cover, format, and everything else, donated more time and talent than I could have afforded otherwise. Bill Schneider of Falcon Press took risks in underwriting it. The staff of the Montana Historical Society patiently answered questions, located microfilm, and repaired overheated photocopiers. Finally, pioneer Montana journalists made *Browsing in the Morgue* a collection I am proud of.

Most journalists, like most other writers and readers, assume that deadline writing belongs in a morgue. By nature it is topical, impulsive, unpolished, and quickly outdated. The writing in nineteenth-century Montana news-papers, for example—partisan, bombastic, libelous—might be of historical interest, might even make good reading, but it is no longer news and most of us assume it never was craftsmanship, "good writing."

As education, technology, and leisure time qualify more people as readers, the market increasingly rewards writers. More people become writers. Writing becomes increasingly emphasized, specialized. Teachers of writing satisfy aspiring writers by defining and sharpening writing skills that can be demonstrated and thus improved. Consensus and criteria naturally emerge. Avoid passive voice. Never say in ten words what you can say in two. More and more good writers collect publications, jobs, royalties, respect.

Meanwhile, readers not only benefit from the general (and undeniable) improvement in writing, but they also frequently suffer. Influenced by writers, readers, too, begin to reject the use of passive voice and wordiness. They, too, learn to delight in a writer's craftsmanship and productivity. But these are criteria of good writing, *not good reading*.

Why insist on the distinction between good reading and good writing? Because readers, with less justification than writers, too often assume that good reading depends on good writing. But the fact that craft can be taught and mastered through practice simply underlines the fact that luck, circumstance, the past, the future, and a thousand other variables which affect both writing and reading *cannot* be taught or controlled. A writer, of course, concentrates on those matters he can influence. But why should a reader assume a writer's limitations? A writer, for example, cannot control history and so she refuses to depend on it. But why should a reader of Adolph Hitler's crudely conceived and written *Mein Kampf* ignore the power, blood, drama, and terrible significance injected into that book by capricious history? What makes *Hamlet* better reading?

Whether writers like it or not, good reading involves far more than good writing. And the selections in *Browsing in the Morgue,* I trust, make excellent reading. Not only are many of them excellently written, but they also were all written by Montanans, about our home and our history, and if they hold less interest for readers in Los Angeles or New York, so what? We can appreciate reading that an ornery stranger "was expostulated with" because we are intimately familiar with the adventurous, decisive, and strong-willed Montana pioneers who never shrank from using that passive voice. We need not be embarrassed by flowery phrases punctuated with terms like "matutinal meal" or "abequatulated" or "a specimen of the genus hobo" because we all remember, even if only second-hand and vaguely, a slower day when the average reader spent more than 7.6 minutes with the newspaper, when the printed word did not compete with photographs, film, television, or recorded music to entertain and educate us. And we cheat ourselves if we always demand genius of our reading—a straightforward explanation of the weather flags our grandparents relied on is more satisfying, more enriching in many ways than a perfect poem.

In short, good writing often disappoints us but good reading, by definition, never does. Some of us prefer clippings to classics. We relish anonymous Montana editors, whose brash newspapers and towns died long ago, while we bashfully avoid immortals like Milton, Shakespeare, or Updike. Other readers choose avant-garde fiction or rhymed devotional verses or survivalist manuals, and someday we may, too. But for now, while we browse in the morgue, our tastes are above reproach. Writers, after all, do not call us—we call them.

We, as readers, raise them from the dead.

Missoula Gazette, January 16, 1889

x

COMEDIES
"A cheerful if not more so, aspect"

FROM EMIGRANT GULCH.

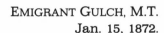

EMIGRANT GULCH, M.T.
Jan. 15, 1872.

Things and other matters in this region of mountains, dales, trout and other suckers, are assuming a cheerful if not more so, aspect. The Apollo bosom of the Hon. Jed. Crooks, swells with pride as he beholds in the shadowy distance heaps of honors to be piled upon him by the Lost Tribe of Israel—the noble band of the As-souts. But to explain. Once upon a time, several years ago, might have been seen here a prosperous mining camp—but it was not seen. A few hardy, and some hardier cusses lit on this spot and commenced the search for the unalloyed article. Old Dame Fortune smiled upon them, but Old Dad "Poker" scowled, and the boys "went through" plenty. Times became hard, and a change came over the spirits of their dreams, and times became harder. The denizens of Emigrant became disheartened and waxed thin. Now turn we to their brethern, the Crows.

Congress in its enlightened spirit saw the noble reds wandering without military escort, and so therefore in accordance with a wise Public policy, they herded the chivalric red boys; built for them a corral—an Agency—near unto the settlements of the ruffianly whites, in order that they might not be discommoded by long journeying after the scalps of the latter. The Crows of the Govt. got up and grew fat, the As-souts of Emigrant went down and grew thin.

Now become we more explicit. The following minutes of a big medicine talk of the As-souts, as handed me by the big Secretary, Spouty Anderson, explains itself or at least should do so:

BIG MEDICINE LODGE, EMIGRANT GULCH,

(Forgot the date.)

Council met and called to order. Big Chief Windy Wood on the barrel. Minutes of last meeting lost, consequently not read. No objection made to the minutes.

Rummy Doughty, Little Medicine Man presented for the consideration of the Council several pints. Vote of thanks tendered to Rummy for the same. The Council took a recess for the purpose of taking under consideration and their vests said pints. Called to order. Stumpy Glitten, Big Medicine Man, proposed inasmuch as our noble band were growing strong, to petition Congress, pray that we be set on a reservation, or be joined to the Crows. Striker Clifford, War chief was strongly opposed to said pray. On invitation, Sachems, Beans and Offman, of the Crows, said they would do all in their power to aid their brethern and sling their marks to the Petition. Bully, for them. Took another recess. Recessed for one hour. Yerman Fred. proposed to send the Petition through our Bozeman Father, Horatio N. Micawber, or some similar name. Cries of "Bully for Mack. and Clark's Fork." Upon motion, the Secretary drew on the Treasurer for seven dollars and six bits, for irrigating fixins. Recessed, and sampled the fluid.

Upon motion it was resolved to have a big war dance when the Petition was completed.

Professor Orahood was invited to act as poet and sling his favorite epic—"We won't slop over till morning," and also to deliver an ode.

Objection raised because he *owed* enough already. Objection not sustained.

A young tragedian was invited to deliver "the Sailor Boy's Dream."

A Bozeman singist was invited to sing "Shamus O'Brien," and execute a hop.

Col. Gardiner was requested to do the music but as his violin was broken, it was proposed to take it out in whistling.

The Hon. Geo. Crooks was invited to sit at the second table, his eating powers being well known to the Council.

Recessed and sampled.

Several motions tabled. Rummy Doughty, Striker Clifford, "slopped over" and were placed under the table. Motion—accepted, adjourned, next meeting, *sine die.* Petition, Bully—Don't care if I do.

SPOUTY ANDERSON,

Secretary.

The latter portion of the minutes must have been of a secret session, hence their ambiguity. I now append the great Petition, signed by over three hundred, for I know such to be the case, for I saw Spouty Anderson sign them.

COUNCIL WIGWAM OF THE AS-SOUTS,

Third Moon, 18th Quarter.

To the Hon. the House of Representatives and the Senate of the U.S., in Heap Big Tepee assembled.

Your Petitioner, chief of which Big Chief Windy Woods, is whom, would represent to your honorable bodies, that we are for the greater part, orphans—far from home, with all its endearing charms, and pray that you would stretch your arms over us in a protecting manner and not snatch us bald-headed.

We would pray that we be placed on probation and when ascertained that we are as good as the Crows, then like them, give us our daily rations.

We would further pray that as coats, socks, tooth picks and paper collars are furnished the Crows, that we receive the same, and not in lieu thereof—breech clouts.

The Crows have Needle-guns and we pray that we be furnished with flint-locks.

We further pray and pray strong that a Professor be sent amongst the Crows for the purpose of establishing a chair of

3

Poker in the Yellowstone University. This placing them in point of learning on an equality with us.

We further pray loud that our boundaries may extend to the Gallatin valley, Taylor's Bridge, head of Wind River, and including Salt Lake, providing McKean gets away with the Mormons. This last we emphatically pray for as our squaws are not numerous.

Your Petitioners further pray that the leading spirits of the As-souts be given high positions, such as army officers and Indian agents, several of us being willing to qualify for the latter by joining the Quakers, or Methodists, or both.

We further pray that the Hon. Jed. Crooks be given a position as stone artist, at Sing Sing.

We also pray, and this time very loud, that any little or big favors lying around loose may be conferred upon our noble band—in the event of your refusing, may you be d——d and your Petitioners will ever pray etc.

WINDY WOODS,
Big Chief.

Here you have the doings of this noble band. Soon I will waft to you how the As-souts are wagging.

In the *interim* I patiently wait, and sigh for the good time coming when Congress will recognize my brilliant qualities, and confer upon me a galorious posish.

Chiefly Thine,
HON. JED. CROOKS.

The Avant Courier (Bozeman), February 1, 1872

—The other night a stranger appeared in a down town saloon and created a panic among those present by eating a $5 bill. He was expostulated with for his extravagant act and rewarded his advisers with eating a $10 bill under the pretense that he could eat his own money if he wanted to. The police locked him up.

Rocky Mountain Celt (Butte-Anaconda), March 4, 1899

THE HON. JED CROOKS EXPERIENCES TROUBLE.

His Article Concerning a Certain Tribe Meets With Disapproval.

The former tranquility and general repose of my mind has undergone a severe shock. The faultless symmetry of this noble form has been damaged much, if not mucher. These classic features which have thrown savage scowls upon adversaries, and beamed forth—of July smiles upon the fair, is now covered with hieroglyphics, which would baffle the researches of that British antiquarian who is "best up" in the inscriptions on the Pyramids to decipher.

I assume a longitudinal position in order to explain.

The time was yesterday, somewhere between the longitude of breakfast and supper.

I had hashed but once when I saw coming in the direction of Emigrant Gulch, several representatives from the noble Emigrant Tribe. Onward they came. With visible emotions, and a patent palpitating bosom, I slung out my digits in welcome to the noblest Roman of them all. He cast aside my proffered hand, and in geyser tones asked of me my name. With pride I gave it unto him. "You wrote an account of our big medicine meeting," (half interrogatory). I smilingly nodded an affirmative nod. "Square yourself," he thundered in mud volcanic notes. I blandly informed him that in consequence of not being "well up" in Geometry, and taking into consideration that I was a few inches taller than broad, that the problem of *squaring myself* was one which my weak intellect could not grapple with. "Won't you do it?" he yelled in a husky corned breath. "I give it up," I falteringly said.

Now followed a scene which was chiefly characterized by its general carelessness and extreme reckless looseness.

My interviewer very feelingly "let out " with his left duke,

5

but I instantly stopped its progress with my starboard eye, and—then sat down.

I now had a faint suspicion that the gentleman who had the floor entertained the design (as one of his compatriots poetically remarked), "to lick me."

I arose and lunging out with my right chief of staff, just as my opponent stepped to side, and had the satisfaction of "knocking out of time," the stove drum, and depositing myself on top of the heated cast iron outfit. Some one called "time," I wished to know if he referred to bed-time, as I was "Oh so weary, mother, dear." I then took out that loose tooth and gave it to the valued friend who did the picking up business for me. I can hardly realize the fact that my opponent's eye is looking gloomy—is encircled with a halo of blue, liken unto as if an indigo bag had been reposing there or thereabouts. My cheeks become suffused, and I am deposited in a tangled situation in a corner. I unwind my lower limbs, and slinging upwards my right boot hit my antagonist somewhere; cries of "foul"; I blush while thinking of my hose.

The impromptu referee decides that the friendly strife must go on. I throw out both my dukes, when two zephyr-like taps are felt, one on my proboscis, the other on my own eye, while my Webster head seeks blissful repose in a tin spittoon.

I look around, but see nothing. The sponge goes up. I receive the congratulation of friends, and kindly allow my late opponent to make any apologies he desires to in the premises.

A deputation of the tribe condole with me and hope that I will recover soon, as they wish each of them to have "a bout" with me.

Now, as a fightist, I am good, but my business duties compel me to forego the anticipated pleasure of having my eyes closed and my snoot busted.

Please state that I will be absent until after Christmas—I have business on the Upper Yellowstone—I must away to the geysers—Farewell—Jed Crooks *has gone a' geysering.*

HON. JED CROOKS.

The Avant Courier (Bozeman), February 15, 1872

FROZEN.

A party who keeps a saloon about two miles from Virginia, had a greater run of custom than usual one night lately. Finding that he was liable to get out of whisky he kept adding water to his stock at intervals. The boys who had imbibed the night before feeling pretty dry the next morning, went to the saloon for their "bitters," but judge of their astonishment and disgust on finding that the "torchlight procession" had been dilated to such an extent that it was frozen solid in the bottle. The boys said nothing, but silently stole away for a happier clime where a supply of tarantula juice could be had.

The Montana Capital Times (Virginia City), April 9, 1870

RED LODGE CORRESPONDENCE.

"A Daniel come to judgment."—*Shylock.*

Ole Upthe Kreekson was up before the court a few days ago on the charges of intemperance, disturbing the peace, and trying to run the town. The case attracted some attention as it was rumored that the judge had decided to place his No. 11 cowhides on such diversions, and to deal firmly with all offenders against the public peace. It may be appropriate to remark right here that his honor had retired from public life during the holiday season, and in a lonely retreat his humble heart found that peace of mind and feeling of rest denied those whose life is passed mid scenes of toil and strife, sin and sorrow; while there communing with nature and other kindred and ardent spirits he formed the high and lofty resolve to eradicate from our midst all elements of strife and unnatural excitement, to the end that our community may become a model of peace and harmony, that we may love our neighbor but not his wife, and that even our social club may fulfill the literal meaning of its appellation. With his usual discernment he reasoned that the first attack must be made on the root or rather spring of all evil, and following the dictates of his mind he charged on the fiery fiend, made prisoner of all he could get at, and with unswerving zeal and pertinacity proceeded to down it. His efforts were eminently successful, oceans of strife stirring fluid were absorbed, and the supply becoming exhausted, his honor turned his judicial mind toward seeking offenders who were still able to get at the vile stuff he had labored to destroy.

Hearing faint rumors of the above intentions the citizens of our town thronged to the temple of justice to attend the trial of Mr. Kreekson. The court having convened it was charged that the prisoner had been boisterous and unruly, that his conduct was calculated to intimidate the timid, and was unbecoming a gentleman and subject of the czar. For the defense Mr. Kreekson stated that on the evening in question he was at the popular resort of Mr. "Careless," intent only on seeing the elephant; that while gazing with open jaws on the glittering faro tables he was approached by no less a personage than his honor on the bench, who demanded that he (the prisoner) should forthwith set 'em up, and that there was laid the foundation of his trouble. The court arose slowly and impressively, his face bore an expression that would strike terror to a wild-cat, as he announced that the prisoner was guilty of gross contempt of court and in proceeding to dilate on the enormity of the offence he grew excitable and nervous. Presently assuming a theatrical attitude, his honor stared at a vacant portion of the room and questioned thusly. "Is that a serpent of Hell or goblin damned?" The attorney for the defence informed his honor that he must see some large sized snakes, and stated that in his own experience they were more familiar as they insinuated their slimy folds within his boots. The sheriff endeavored to preserve order, and assure the court, failing he grasped his honor, and rushing to a barrel of pure Rock creek that stood in the corner he stuck the judge in and proceeded to soak his head. After being taken out his honor was evidently cooled off and expressed his thanks to the sheriff for introducing him to a liquid he had not known internally, or externally since his baptism.

The court having resumed his place on the bench the trial proceeded, and Mr. Kreekson being found guilty of succumbing to the influence of his libations without sufficient provocation, was fined, the fine being paid the prisoner was purged of contempt by withdrawing his previous remark and stating that the judge offered to set 'em up first.

The court adjourned and as the judge, attorney for defence, and their friends were passing I heard his honor casually remark, as he jingled the proceeds of the fine in his pocket, "Boys, I am weary and thirsty, I must go and find the Duke."

As I plodded homeward I meditated on the future possibilities of a people who showed their hand by electing his honor to the bench. Verily, sayeth I, being elected by popular vote his honor must be a true representative of his district.

SNOWBALL.

Red Lodge, Jan. 12, 1891.

The Billings Gazette, January 15, 1891

—I heard a good story about a Montana judge of the early days. He was sentencing a half-breed prisoner, when the latter drew a knife and brandishing it at the judge shouted "You're no good, I hold the law in my hand." The judge reached down under his desk and pointing a horse-pistol at the half-breed said, "And I hold the Constitution." The prisoner saw that there was no use trying to get the "Constitution" amended, so he accepted the decision with brutal grace.

Great Falls Tribune, September 11, 1886

THE BACHELOR'S FIEND.

Written for the INTER-LAKE.

By J.E. RICHARDSON.

What makes the bachelor's life a curse?
What makes him go from bad to worse?
What theme weighs down my heavy verse?
   Sour dough bread.

What makes his morning meal a dread?
What makes him linger in his bed,
While holding in both hands his head?
   Sour dough bread.

What, when the sun with noonday heat,
Proclaims 'tis time for men to eat;
What makes him turn with faltering feet?
   Sour dough bread.

When supper time returns again,
In summer, winter, sunshine or rain,
What chants he still in sad refrain?
   Sour dough bread.

When, on his couch he seeks repose,
And short surcease from all his woes,
What spectre on his vision grows?
   Sour dough bread.

And often in the doleful night
What makes him yell out in affright,
Thinking old Nick has got him tight?
   Sour dough bread.

If when in town he wets his lip,
What makes the earth roll like a ship,
And try its best his feet to trip?
   Sour dough bread!!

What gives him all next day the hyp?
What holds his hair with such a grip?
What swears he then, he'll never sip?
   Sour dough bread!!!

What vampire foul absorbs his money?
What steeps in gall his sweetest honey?
What turns his thoughts to matrimony?
Sour dough bread!

And when he's laid upon his bier,
And men shall ask: "What brought him here?"
What answer comes, in accents drear?
Sour dough bread!

What makes with hate my bosom swell?
What makes me feel like murder fell?
What makes me write this doggerel?
Sour dough bread.

Oh, curse thee! curse thee! walleyed spook!
Curse thee, by candle, bell and book!
Curse thee, each time I have to cook—
Sour dough bread!!!!!

The Inter-Lake (Demersville), February 21, 1890

THE KNOCKER.

In introducing the KNOCKER to the public I have no apology to make. I am not out for any particular good, but hope that I may benefit some one and that one may be myself.

If any mistakes have crept into my form or make up, lay them where they belong, as I plead not guilty, owing to the fact that I enjoyed none of the pleasures of my conception, nor suffered the pains of my birth. I am what I am, no more, no less, and such I shall make the KNOCKER, free and independent.

We all carry our own sky with us and we get out of this world just what we put in it. As for myself, I have put so little in this terrestrial sphere I do not expect to reap a very bounteous harvest.

While I do not consider it my business to dip into the

secrets of married life, nor thoroughly explore the jungles, neither do I intend to do any free advertising to show where shame can be purchased at the lowest rate. The KNOCKER I intend to make a good, live, readable paper, containing all the news that will be of interest to its patrons. I will play no favorites, as "all coons look alike to me."

Having been in this world for the past 29 years, I have seen nearly all the phases of life from the cradle to the gates of hell, and I have learned that a man's best friend is his pocketbook, but even then he wants some of the filthy lucre in that book.

The cold and chilly winds of adversity have blown through my whiskers so long that I hardly know what I would do should the sunlight of prosperity happen to shine upon my path. But like all others, I am willing to gamble and take a chance.

It might be well to give notice in advance that all libel suits are declared off and that it would be useless to try and whip the editor, who happens to be myself, as I am something of a foot racer and have already demonstrated this fact.

In politics the KNOCKER will be strictly independent, wearing no man's collar nor tied to the apron strings of any political grandmother. Free silver will be the watchword and the freer it is showered upon your humble servant the better he will like it.

In religion the KNOCKER will worship at the shrine of the Almighty Dollar, believing that prayers said in the editorial sanctorium are just as good as those offered up by the preachers in the pulpit at so much a shot.

While it has often been reported that Dame Fortune knocks once upon a man's door, I believe that her daughter, Miss Fortune, steals a march on the old lady and gets around more often. The old woman is good enough for me, and I am willing to stuff the daughter off to some of the younger bloods who have more time left to waste in this world of vice and expectations.

Trusting that my salutatory will not be my valedictory, I remain

Yours Truly,
JOSEPH J.G. BURNS,
Editor the KNOCKER.

The Belt Knocker, December 10, 1897

LEM HILL'S FUNERAL.

Another of the queer characters in White Horse camp was a man known as Lem Hill. He was as mild as buttermilk and as dull as a hoe, and no one ever thought of asking his advice or interesting themselves in his affairs. One day he took sick, and after a period lasting about three weeks it was seen that he must die. It was deemed best that some one should break the news to him, and so "Judge" Kelso dropped in and said:—"Lem, you are goin' to turn up your toes before another sunrise."

The judge didn't mean to be sudden or unfeeling, but that was his way.—"I guess I am," quietly replied Lem. "Well, that pint being settled and no exceptions taken, what last requests hev ye got to make? We want to do the fair thing, you know, although it's a busy time."—"Kin I hev a funeral?" queried Lem.—"You kin."—"Reg'lar procession?"—"Yes."—"I don't expect any coffin, of course, but I'd like to hev the affair pulled off reasonably decent. You kin plant me on the hill beside the Frenchman. I guess we won't quarrel."—"Yes we'll do that, though it's purty hard digging up thar."—"Needn't mind going over a couple of feet," said Lem, "and the fellers with the body had better take the left-hand path as they go up; it's easier to climb."

"Got any wealth?" asked the judge after a moment's silence.—"A couple of ounces, mebbe."—"Mighty slim show for a big spread on that, but we can't help it. Well, Lem, it's my busy day, you know, and I must cut this short. Hope you won't take offense."—"Oh, certainly not; don't neglect work on my account. Sunthin said at the grave?"—"Jist a few words, Lem, and I'll say 'em myself. I'll practice up this afternoon, and get some whiskey to clear my throat. I want to make a decent job of it."—"What'll you say?"—"Why, that you died happy—hev left an aching void—we shall all miss you—cut down in your prime. I'll lay it on purty thick."

"Well, I'm sure I couldn't ask for more and perhaps it's better than I could expect. So long, judge. Go back to your work, and I'll go on with my dying." And the judge left the shanty whistling as was his wont, and Lem had been dead over an hour before word came to us down in the gulch. The funeral came off the next morning, and it has always been a pleasant remembrance with me that the judge did considerable better than he agreed to. He gave two eulogies in place of one, and after the burial he licked one of the men who wouldn't knock off work to attend.

Jefferson County Sentinel (Boulder), July 12, 1889

WHEELS IN HIS HEAD.

◄●►

A Livingston Stone Mason
Has a Defective Mental Foundation.

◄●►

A Livingston stone mason named Snoddy is off his trolley again and has been recommitted to the insane asylum at Warm Springs. He was adjudged insane over a year ago, but recovered his reason after an incarceration of some eight months. The first time he went crazy he was found whirling around on his head in a newly plowed field and had buried himself up to his shoulders. He imagined he was up on a big Ferris wheel and told a wonderful story of what he imagined he had seen up among the clouds. He said he followed the path of the sun and found out all about the mysterious workings of nature. Said he: "It is the most wonderful sight mortal man ever beheld." He was discharged as cured last fall, but his wheels are now running in all directions again. This time, according to the Livingston correspondent of the Anaconda STANDARD, the unfortunate fellow's mania takes on a religious cast, and he imagines that he is possessed of a good and evil spirit which are constantly at war to obtain the mastery over him. He also imagines that a cat's "mind" has taken possession of his throne of reason and thus deprived him of the mental faculties of a human being.

The Billings Gazette, March 13, 1896

"SENSATION DRAMA."

SCENE.—*West Main st., "by the old cabin door." Time, midnight. Enter (from the Free Concert saloon down Last Chanch Gulch) a lady most used the lager beer glass to handle, and with her a practicioner behind the bar.*

LADY. My window is broken. Alas! what panes taking villain has taken the pains to break my pane. I fear me all is not well within, so I pray you, sir, step in. I will steel my heart against all fear while we stealthily search, and see if some one has not stolen in and something stolen out.

P.B. I'll do it! And if it so chance that I do find a spoiler here, who hath sought to spoil thy goods, then will I his picture spoil, for I am spoiling for a fight.

Both enter.

LADY. What heard I? Was't the tread of the heartless intruder, or merely the trembling of this fluttering heart? Methinks,—I know not what I think!

P.B. Calm your fears, lady. 'Twas but the night wind stealing through the open pane, "only this, and nothing more."

A candle (star brand, St. Louis) is lighted.

LADY. Why, what a joke! The air seemed heavy with ill omens, but now this flame doth show me that my fears have given to "airy nothingness a local habitation and a name."

A noise is heard in the direction of the chimney.

BOTH *(Una Voce).* What's that?

P.B. It is a mouse, caught in some foul trap, who doth, with low squeal, give utterance to his agony.

LADY. Say not so! Methinks those sounds come not from quadrupedal lungs, but that they are the low base tones of the base viol-ator of my abode. Let's seek him; and if we find him, then will we play upon him such a medley of tunes that he shall not know whether he be sounding forth a fandango or a dead march!

P.B. Hark that note! 'Tis A flat, and soundeth in the chimney. Let's for't.

LADY. Agreed! Now heaven help us, and beneath the raspings of my beau (bow) may that note soon change—B flat.

Both gaze up the chimney.

P.B. By heavens! Those biped limbs which do apart distend themselves and embrace the sooty sides of this contracted dome, do so remind me of a man that, faith, I think a man must be above them. A torch, good lady, and quickly will we have a fire ablaze, which shall dislodge this pair of legs, and show unto us what manner of man this is that doth so take up his dwelling.

LADY. No, no! I would not burn him. 'T were a pity so to do, for the air would so savor of the broiling that we might no longer dwell here.

Another squeal in the chimney. Its words: "Help me out!"

P.B. He is fast!—*not* swiftly moving, but slowly stopping still. Now will I drag him down to those depths whence most proceed the tormenting flames—down to the place of fire.

He is drawn down as aforesaid.

BOTH (in chorus). Art thou a fiend who from regions far below, come forth at the hour of midnight to fright poor mortals?

P.B. Art thou the ghost of some foul spirit?

LADY. Hast thou just risen from thy bier (beer)?

FIEND. Would that I had! It must admitted be that I have been tight, but the tight was not a jolly one, and never more will I myself disgrace with thus, against my will, re-treating. Why I entered in this ill-fated place I know not, unless—and I think perhaps 'twas so—that the sight of some fair lady here had tempted me to so conceal myself that I might of her obtain a nearer view.

LADY. Then may my deep damnation curse thee. May'st thou find no *ee*'s in thy bier, and may it ever be as black as thy sooty self!

P.B. *(with uplifted hand)*. And may thy life be one eternal vomit of foul spirits, ejected forth from the open door of thy sick mouth, even as I eject thee from the door of this fair lady's house.

Exit Fiend, a trail of soot behind him, his last words—

16

Do with me as you will. Consult the high dignitaries of the law. E'en bring my poor body before the Duke, and let great Desbeck hurl down anathemas upon this smutty head; but one boon I pray thee grant—I ask but this: let no lisp of yours bring the news of this night's unpleasantness to the knowledge of ye Local of the HERALD!

The curtain drops. A delighted audience applauds the spirited representation of life in Helena, and the band plays a new composition prepared expressly for the occasion by some musical prospectors, entitled, "The Chimney, or A Blow Out on the Bar Keep Lead!"

Helena Daily Herald, November 13, 1867

ANOTHER CANDIDATE.

ORRTOWN, (wich is in the Keounty of Bighorn,)
March 20, 1867.

To the head of the Beaver News.—Dear and fraternal sir.

Seein by yer papers that a grate many of the citizens in this grate gold barin communitie, are sendin their autergrafs in as candidates fur goin tew the House of Rips, I will give yew a few remarks as'll have a tendency to rise my gud caractur, and these few remarks are regardin myself; my natur is kinder solemcolly in this beautiful keountry, I am only sixtie years of age, lackin a few, I was bornd in the Stait of Missouri, and am skilled in Graymaticle frazes, I stand ten feet, five, in my stockin feet. I beg pardin for the above, caus the above remark is intended fur five feet, ten inches. I rite this so yooul understand I am not a giantic cuss, I have one wife sixtie years older an I be so yew see I'm all wright; she sais she'd like ter go ter Washingtown, and she further sais she'd like ter have me go, tew, not fur the purpus of gettin sum munay, but to dew the Keountry sum gud deal of gud. An I tole her I wud try miscil with the Beaver News printed in Ginier; these fiew remarks I hope are not fencive tew uer

17

eies. If yew succeed in this plot ile send yew the first speech I mak, Ime a gud speaker, and havent the least objection to belongin tew the House of Rips.

SADANAPALUS RODUM, candidate fur House of Rips.

P.S. (wich is postscript) He rite a fiew lines weeklie and in my next ile describe the hansum sitty of Orrtown, wich is in the Keounty of Bighorn.

Beaver Head News (Virginia City), March 26, 1867

THE WHISKY CURE.

This Column is Taking the Whisky Cure.

Dipsomania is what the doctors call the drink habit. It can be cured like any other disease. The proper remedy applied with patience brings the answer every time. Patience and the proper remedy are just the middle names for the Billings Whisky Cure.

Some people say it costs too much, but that is a scarecrow of the imagination. Four treatments per day for three weeks is equal to eighty-four visits from the doctor, and where is the Billings doctor who lets you off at one dollar a trip? Show!

Typhoid fever, rheumatism, child-birth cost more than the whisky cure if they last as long.

When a man comes to the jumping off place and finds that he is going down into a hog's nest for the balance of his life if he does not reform, it is time to reform.

Going into partnership with the whisky devil is risky business. The silent partner is liable to cheat the other fellow out of all the money he has in the concern. What is the use of hanging onto the devil's tail after he has skinned you? You only hurt business by standing around like a circus poster on the fence, to attract attention.

An old-time republican once gave this advice to his son, who believed in free wool: It may be hard to believe, my boy, but there are some smarter things in this world than you are. Look at the sheep!

In every town in the United States somebody has been cured of the whisky habit by this new fangled whisky cure, so there must be something in it. It seems to be needed everywhere except in Heaven, and all Montanians who expect to take in the latter place should get their baggage checked and make the other necessary preparations. Since the World's Fair is closed there is no place else to go. There is no license system there and the whisky cure may not be doing business when you pass in your chips.

Every man in the universe has a right to do as he pleases, if his wife will let him. Don't make a drink fiend of your self because somebody else does. The other man may be laughing at you to keep his courage up, or maybe he don't have the money to blow in for the whisky cure.

Here is one of them Florida allegories, as an old lady said in the fisheries building at the World's Fair. A man who had a strong appetite for whisky put it into training for several years and made a regular John L. Sullivan of it. It got to be so strong that it led the man around by the nose. He finally took it with him to see the Billings Whisky Cure, which is away ahead of Corbett when it comes to knocking out whisky. All the preliminaries were arranged and a set-to was commenced between the principals. In a few days it became evident that the man's whale of an appetite for hot stuff was not so fat, ragged and sassy as it was last week. After several more days he refused to walk up to the counter and take his medicine as he once did. This surprised the man's friends, because it was a treat. Later the man smelled the cork of a beer bottle and then went out. He came back shortly and told the man with the cork that he had robbed him of fifty cents. The cork man said he was mistaken and they both went out in the yard and saw the square meal that Sullivan had eaten lying on the cold, cold ground. The gate receipts went to the winner, of course.

Tobacco Cure	$25.00
Whisky Cure	50.00
Morphine Cure	75.00

J.E. FREE

The Billings Gazette, January 20, 1894

THE REASON.

A request for a New Year's poem elicited the following
from a contributor of the TRIBUNE.

Alone he sat at the break of day
  In his cabin alone and drear.
Sleep had not come its tribute to pay
  The last night of the dying year.

His heart was sad, as he looked back
  On the year, and on years before.
As over the past he revived the track
  Of his wand'rings, so long and sore.

The faces of those he loved at home
  Came up, passed in fond review,
The father who warned him not to roam
  And his mother, so loving and true.

The brothers, then boys, now grown up men
  Had remained through all the years
His sisters, the girls, he called them then
  Women, with wives' hopes and fears.

How is it with him this new year morn
  This day of the holiday wish,
Why is he sad, and why does he mourn
  What's the cause of his soul's anguish?

Do his thoughts of home depress him so
  Have his wanderings such an effect
As to make him hold his head so low?
  No, it's not that, I hardly suspect.

With the last iron dollar his partner went
  For a bottle of budge to the store.
Outside lies the partner badly bent,
  The bottle broke, just in front of the door.—

Yours cheerfully,
Y.H. TIMS.

Great Falls Tribune, January 1, 1887

A New Arrival—A mule skinner came to town and fired up last night, and imagined that some one was imposing on him. He dropped into a saloon and jumping up and down gave a few war whoops, saying, "I am the man that ketched a wild broncho on the Inyan-Kara, and helt him till his chin come out. I can lick a room full of wild cats and mountain lions with nothing but a jack knife to fight with, and I can dance a jig on the pint of a copper lightning rod. I ain't liable to cold, but when I sneeze the report'rs telegraph a fresh earthquake in Cuby; when I give a war whoop the dishes rattle on the Russian King's table till old Gotchermolikichihoph swears that a keg of nihilist gunpowder has just popped in the cellar, and the empress has to hunt her new teeth from her coffee cup. Give me some beer!" This time he struck the counter with his fist a terrific blow, causing the glasses to rattle, at which point the bar-keep interposed an injunction in the way of a stunning blow between the eyes, causing the nasal organ to give forth a considerable amount of the ruby fluid, and his general appearance indicated that he was badly rattled.

The Yellowstone Journal (Miles City), May 22, 1880

A POCKETBOOK.

A small, innocent looking pocketbook, firmly nailed to the walk in front of the Montana, afforded considerable amusement for an hour yesterday afternoon to those who were "inside." It was really surprising to observe the antics of men of wealth and social position when the "loaded" purse caught their eyes. They would hesitate in their walk with a "will I yield to the tempter" expression, start up suddenly as if it had just occurred to them how unseemly it might appear, and then, with a long, graceful reach, swipe the "morocco" bank. In the meantime Rod Williams, Wade Chilcott, Tighe Wellcome and several others were taking in the proceedings from the "inside." But some of the victims lost all control of themselves when they saw the holder of trash. Frank Kennedy and L.W. Katzenstein came up Main street together, and both "saw it first." They made a regular Brodie plunge for it, landing in a bunch on top of the much abused book. Jim Berry, Joe Carroll, S.S. Raymond, James Chambers, D.J. Fitzgerald, Joe Walsh and two Cree Indians were among those who bit the dust.

Joe Carroll intended to start yesterday afternoon for his old home, Louisiana, Mo., but he hurt his arm, or at least Dr. Spelman convinced him it was injured, in his attempt to grab the stubborn wallet. Mr. Carroll will leave to-day for Missouri, if nothing happens.

The Anaconda Standard, February 23, 1893

FRIGHTFUL.

An individual of German origin, while wading through the deep snow of Spring Gulch, was startled by the appearance of the Meteor. He declared the next morning, that it passed within two feet of his head.

Another individual who saw it, said he thought it a fitting representation of the Extra Session; momentary brilliant, but exploding into utter darkness, the places which knew it, knowing it no more, forever.

Still another thought it was the sun falling from the firmament, to set the world on fire, in pursuance of gospel prophecy.

We have recently visited the scene of the late Extra Session; the explosion was as complete as if it had been effected by Nitro Glycerine. Not a vestige remains. Even the shield and flag are gone. And the members, once so jubilant and happy, where are they? Echo answers WHERE. The Hole in the Wall, through which they passed to take their drinks—the billiard tables whereon they played still remain in the old place, the bar as well supplied as ever, the tables surrounded by as many happy faces. Thus we pass "One generation goeth and another cometh." What is to be the next please? A person who visited the scene immediately after the accident, was fortunate in finding a part of an Original Bill providing for the holding of a territorial election of a delegate to Congress in April. He will submit it to the inspection of Prof. Aggasiz on his arrival in the Territory, to ascertain what manner of creature it belongs to. OH!

Beaver Head News (Virginia City), March 26, 1867

—"Swede Ole" started in on a grand celebration last Saturday. He ingurgitated freely of stagger-juice all day and was, in consequence, in splendid trim for the political jubilee in the evening. He imagined himself Napoleon leading the hosts to victory. Marching at the head of the column Ole waved his unsteady hand and cried "Com a het a du." But Ole was great in peace as well as in imaginary war. At the conclusion of the speeches he delivered an oration, which sparkled with gems of incoherency. He wound up his peroration with "rah fur old Toole war Sanders hoss rah." But Ole is versatile. He was up on conviviality as well as military and eloquence. He followed the boys around town to all the saloons. They tried to down Ole by giving him whisky by the beer glass full, but old Skandinavia would not down. He was a stayer from away back in the old country. But alas, for greatness! Even Ole's great counterpart met his nemesis. Ole's Waterloo was when he tried to light his cigar-stub with a huge fire-brand snatched from the bonfire. He slapped the lighter up against his nose; the latter, surcharged with alcohol, exploded, and poor Ole, first in war, first in peace and last to leave the flowing bowl, was seen no more.

Great Falls Tribune, October 9, 1886

Weekly Inter Mountain (Butte), August 17, 1882

TRAGEDIES
"A chapter of blood"

THE FIRST HANGING.

◄●►

It was down near Rocker that the first hanging within what now constitutes Silver Bow county took place. It was not a judicial execution; nor the carrying out of a decree from the court of Judge Lynch, nor the work of a frenzied mob. It was simply the cool, premeditated act of a disheartened miner who hanged a Chinaman, as he expressed it, "just for luck." It took place in 1868 or '69. The lack of date, or the name of the hangman or his victim does not alter the fact of the hanging, and facts are what it is desired to present herein.

The Chinaman was one among the very few who had drifted over this way from Idaho at that early date. Chinamen are not pioneers in any clime, but they will sometimes closely follow in the wake of the Anglo-Saxon and are satisfied to pick up a little here and a little there of what the white man leaves. They are placer mine scavengers and will work and wash everything from a pile of old tailings to a square of new dirt which once performed the office of sluice supporter, to lay by a dollar or two. They are a patient, industrious people and keep themselves, as much as possible, out of the way of the wheels of progress. Still they work and exhaust the diggings which many of those people who come after them would be glad to mine. Probably this particular Chinaman, who was ushered into the great hereafter, was filling a place in the diggings around Rocker which Dan Haffie thought some Christian gentleman might wish to fill at a future day. Be this as it may, Dan concluded that the interests of white humanity, and the fickleness of his own particular fortune, required a sacrifice of an Indian or a Chinaman. The Indian could not be had and a Chinaman could, so Dan decided that the Celestial must "go."

About a week after Haffie came to this conclusion, an opportunity presented itself to carry out his purpose. The weather was fine; a rope was handy, the Chinaman was alone, a log projected over his cabin and the surroundings were buried in the silence of evening. Approaching the Chinaman, who was enjoying a quiet pipe in the door of his hut, Haffie thus addressed him:

"John, come here, I want to see you."

"Wha for you want to see me?" asked the heathen.

"Come here, I tell you!"

"No, you come here."

Dan went. He was tired of parleying and was hot. With one blow he felled the Chinaman, who lay at his feet like a log. Grasping the senseless form in his Samson-like arms, he partly dragged and partly carried the son of the Orient to the projecting log. In a moment a noose was around his neck; the next the rope was thrown over the projection, and the limp body of John was soon swinging in the air. It was all done in less time than it takes to tell it and the first hanging on Silver Bow creek was completed without judge, jury, or spectators. Whether Dan's luck changed or not is not a matter of record.

Another version of the affair is that Haffie leased some ground to Chinamen. He accused one of them of stealing something from his cabin. The Chinaman denied the charge, but Haffie being convinced of his guilt hanged him and left the country. A man by the name of Collins served a term in the penitentiary for the offense, but was released upon the facts becoming known. That a Chinaman was hanged without judge, jury or sheriff, at Rocker, is a matter of record. The event, however, emphasizes the fact that the crude condition of society, at that early date, made it possible for men who considered themselves aggrieved by the unlawful acts of others, to administer corrective measures without troubling courts or juries with the adjudication of differences wherein Chinamen or petty thieves of any nationality were the offenders. When, in the opinion of the pioneers, society needed protection, the "protection" was forthcoming without hesitation.

Rocky Mountain Celt (Butte-Anaconda), March 11, 1899

A TRUE BEAR STORY.

————◄●►————

A Large Crowd Witnessed the Killing of One in Billings.

————◄●►————

Wednesday afternoon quite a crowd of curious people collected on the vacant lot opposite THE GAZETTE office to witness a novel execution, that of a half grown black bear owned by J.W. Vaughan & Bro. The animal has been in their possession since he was a cub, and was about 18 months old. The owners had no place to keep him and he was becoming troublesome, and as he was fat and in good condition they concluded to sacrifice him to the holiday festivities and utilize the fat juicy steaks his carcass will supply.

Bruin was tied to a telegraph pole, to which was rigged a block and tackle. Then he was thrown by means of a rope attached to one of his legs and his four feet also secured by ropes. With these pulled taut, and another around his neck attached to a telegraph pole, the bear was stretched out in such a manner as to be helpless. B.F. Pinneo played the part of executioner with a butcher-knife, with which he cut the bear's throat, and he was then suspended from the pole by means of the block and tackle. He showed considerable viciousness even after his throat was cut, and it required a second application of the knife to end the brute's agony. The bear weighed about 300 pounds and the skin will be mounted by Taxidermist Soule.

The Billings Gazette, December 22, 1894

WILD AND WOOLY.

◄●►

Samson, the Big Elephant, Inaugurates a Reign of Terror.

◄●►

Assaults His Keeper, Tips Over a Load of Hay and Defies Everybody.

◄●►

Beaten, Shot into and Burned with Red-hot Irons.

◄●►

Samson, Cole's famous elephant, gave a free exhibition on the circus grounds Sunday, and his antics were witnessed by an excited crowd. A large number of people stood about when the five elephants were let out of their monster car, and it was observed that Samson, although he looked as harmless as a fly, was wound about with chains, hobbled and dragging a stick of timber. The keeper told everybody to stand away from this elephant. All five were driven to the water ditch when their peculiar method of drinking was closely watched by the crowd. They then started toward the circus grounds when, without warning, Samson threw his trunk under the faithful horse on which the keeper was seated and both horse and man were thrown violently to the ground. They rolled over in the dust and it was thought for some time they were fatally injured, but such, fortunately, was not the case. This wild elephant then started for a load of hay, put his head against it and over it went. Sam Ferguson, the driver, got out from under the hay and struck out for the foot-hills. The horses started to run away, but were soon caught by the crowd. Samson then struck up the railroad track and the circus attaches came running up from all directions, while the people, now thoroughly excited, kept at a safe distance. The beast went out into the field nearly opposite the round-house, his movements being retarded by the intelligent dog kept with the herd as well as by the circus men. He was finally chained to a telegraph pole and also tied to iron pins that were driven into the ground about him. The men now began beating him to subdue his warlike spirit. They used iron bars, striking him on the trunk, on the muscles of the legs, and wherever he was tender. As fast as they got tired others took up the bars and kept up the warfare. Every few minutes the keeper would ask Samson to speak to him, but the fierce beast still held out. Red-hot irons were brought from the engines and run into Samson's mouth and three charges of buckshot were fired into him. Blood ran out of his mouth and trunk and off his back. He held out nearly two hours, but at last gave the sign of subjection to his keeper, when the chains were loosened and the great animal walked sullenly off to his quarters.

Two hours afterward our reporter was admitted to the tent. Samson stood in the middle of the herd, his eyes nearly closed, occasionally gaping and slowly fanning himself with his big ears. He moved his trunk about as though it were in pain and seemed to be thoroughly subdued. The faithful dog, worn out by the afternoon's battle, lay sleeping at Samson's feet. All who noticed this dog were struck with his remarkably intelligent appearance. He is a true friend of the huge beasts and when asleep they are careful not to step upon him.

Missoula County Times, August 18, 1886

BLOODY MURDER.

◄●►

Joseph Clancy Done to Death Thursday by a Blood-thirsty Vagabond.

◄●►

The Poor Old Man Discovered in His Place Hammered to Death with a Beer Mallet.

◄●►

Three Hobos Arrested, One as Principal, the Other Two as Parties to the Crime.

◄●►

Guilt of John Doe Being Established, a Masked Band of Avengers Break the Jail.

◄●►

The Red Handed Murderer Led to His Doom and Swung from a Telegraph Pole.

◄●►

Thugs, Thieves and Vagabonds Ordered Out and the Town Rid of the Fraternity.

◄●►

The first event in a chapter of blood occurred Thursday afternoon, half an hour after the passenger train pulled out for the west. Of the many villainous looking tramps that have been making a hold out and rendezvous of the vacant buildings in the outskirts of Billings two in particular had by the criminal cast of their countenances attracted attention that day, and shortly after the departure of the train, they

30

being on the platform at the station, struck across to the saloon of Joseph Clancy. An hour afterward it was rumored that Joe Clancy had been held up by some vicious characters and nearly killed. John McCurdy and Geo. Berky arrested one of the men, said to be the principal in the crime and took him down to the jail, and shortly afterward another hard looking character was in the custody of the sheriff. A third one in the precious trio, who had acted as law and order man was arrested and taken to jail as a witness. In the meantime Dr. Chapple had been called to attend Joe Clancy, who was found in his little saloon on Minnesota avenue lying on the floor, his face down, in a pool of blood. Life was extinct before the arrival of the medical man but every means were brought into requisition to restore respiration. The body was laid out and after supper it was intended to conduct the inquest. The three parties to the murder were in custody and inquiry into the circumstances which brought about poor Clancy's death were now in order.

The history of the crime, as told by Wm. Quinn, the last man arrested was that he and the two tramps dropped into Joe Clancy's place to get a drink and sat down at a table. One of the tramps showed money and said he would buy beer and called for a quart. Clancy was alone in the little barroom at the time, and brought the measure out and set it on the table with the three glasses and then asked who was to pay for it. The tramp who called for the beer, John Doe, we will call him as he gave no other name, said he would not pay for it and with a sweep of his arm knocked glasses, measure and all to the floor. Clancy stepped back and picked up the beer mallet and as he did so John Doe struck him a powerful blow in the face which knocked the poor old fellow to the floor in a heap and then picking up the beer mallet, a most formidable weapon, weighing at least twenty pounds, struck the prostrate man a blow in the back of the head which undoubtedly killed him. John Doe became frantic then and stepping up to the silent spectators of the crime asked if they wanted any of it. The man seems to have become a demon after the deed of blood and possibly would not have hesitated to strike down the other two men had they entered any remonstrance. John Doe then went behind the bar and for how long it is not known the tramps had full swing in the saloon and drank several times and tapped the till. Quinn, the ex-sheep herder, had when he first came in deposited a carbine belonging to himself behind the bar, and when the fun was over and the men decided to make tracks he got his gun and as John Doe, the murderer, ran out the back door, he took the front exit and, whether from fear of detection or what is not known, decided to hold up John Doe. This he did just as Berky and McCurdy arrived on the scene and took the murderer down to jail. Berky had seen enough of the row to cause him to obtain a pistol from a neighboring house and come back just in time. The other man who was *particeps criminis* was spotted by Berky and also arrested. He gave his name as Murphy; the murderer was known only by the legal alias of John Doe and the brand of Cain which was on his forehead. The witness, Quinn, gave the above testimony, except as relates to himself, at the inquest held that evening, and it was then decided to continue the inquiry at 10:30 a.m. Friday.

Lynched the Murderer.

Although there had been a growing sentiment of indignation and execration of the deed of blood by which Joe Clancy's life had been taken and his two little children doubly orphaned, the sheriff, although hearing rumors to that effect, did not anticipate any trouble that night, nor that a band of masked and determined avengers would demand the delivery into their tender mercies of the red handed murderer. The sheriff was not prepared to receive them when at the witching hour of night the summons rang out. People in the neighborhood say it was between midnight and 2 o'clock when they were awakened by the noise of powerful blows on what sounded like steel casements. Gib Lane was awakened by the noise and as the moon was very bright could from his dwelling distinguish a crowd of moving figures about and around the jail, patroling the block and challenging all approaching persons, who having their slumbers thus rudely disturbed came out to see what was going on. A number of gentlemen who had been attending a dance congregated as near the scene of action as the masked guards would permit, but no attempt was made at rescue. Sheriff Ramsey says he was surprised at the first call but knew at once what was wanted. Strong in the belief that the Pauley cells and cages would successfully resist all attempts at battering them down with such means as a vigilance committee could bring to bear, and that daylight would intervene and save his prisoners, he denied having the keys, which according to the TIMES he had thrown down the well. After some further parleying the sheriff removed his family and the vigilantes had full swing.

The next event on record was a silent march from the jail to the place of execution where a telegraph pole on the Northern Pacific right of way was selected as the gallows tree, and before the light of day paled the stars a ghastly shape was swinging in the breeze, and an unknown murderer had gone to meet his maker. Twelve hours after the brutal murder of Joseph Clancy, one at least of the murderers had paid the price. The body remained as the avengers left it until about 8 o'clock a.m. when by order of Coroner Chapple it was cut down and turned over to the undertaker.

An inquest was held upon the body in the forenoon, the jury being Fred Sweetman, foreman, W.F. Strait, G.A. Robinson, A. Fenton, James Chapple and W.A. Boots. The verdict they returned has been recorded in similar cases thousands of times, "We the jury find that the deceased came to his death by hanging at the hands of party or parties unknown to the jury." There was no mark of identification about the body, no letters or papers or money. Some anguished heart may pine for knowledge of his fate but it is better as it is. Whether or not he made a confession, told his true name, made any ante mortem statement or dying request cannot be learned; the actors in the last party which John Doe attended decline to make themselves known and refuse to be interviewed.

Joseph Clancy.

Later in the day (Friday) than had been intended, owing to the occurrences of the night, the inquest over the body of Joseph Clancy, the tramps' victim, was resumed. This jury, consisting of A.P. Hart, W.H. Ross, James Kelly, P. Ovren, J.S. Conners and A.J. Gilsdorf, after viewing the remains Thursday and taking the testimony of Quinn, now heard additional evidence. The other tramp, Murphy, gave in his testimony which in the main corroborated Quinn's statement. Other testimony was heard and the jury brought in the verdict, "that the deceased met his death at the hands of John Doe, whose real name is to the jury unknown, who did in cold blood and feloniously murder him."

Joseph Clancy was one of the oldest settlers of the town and in early days had charge of the coal docks for the railroad company at Billings. He was about 50 years of age, a widower with two small children, his wife having died about two years ago. Joe was scarcely able to be about at the time of the assault upon him, and had been bed-ridden and under the doctor's treatment for several months. His death from natural causes would have been no surprise at any time recently. The funeral arrangements were undertaken by the Maverick Hose company, Joe Clancy having been one of the pioneer members of the company and entitled to wear the veteran's medal. The funeral took place Saturday afternoon, the Mavericks attending in a body, and the fire bell tolling, with the flag on the Fire hall drooping at half mast. It was probably the largest funeral procession that has for many a year taken its solemn way to the Billings cemetery.

Good Riddance of Bad Rubbish.

Friday morning after the lynching of Clancy's murderer the vagabonds, hobos and criminals that had counted themselves safe in harbor when Billings was reached, poured out from their hiding places like rats from a sinking ship and stayed not upon the order of their going but went at once. Twenty-eight of this bad element crossed the railroad bridge across the Yellowstone before the sun up and in a few hours the town was well rid of them. Murphy and Quinn, the other actors in the Clancy murder were ill-advisedly turned loose after the inquest on Clancy had been finished and warned to make good use of the time left for them to get out of town. Murphy went west and Quinn made tracks toward the rising sun and had progressed as far as Glendive Sunday and had been ordered out of that town. It is believed that Billings will be annoyed no more by the gang for some months. Saturday night a report was current that an army of hobos had gathered at the bridge and were waiting for midnight to swoop down upon the town and avenge the lynching of their comrade by the citizens brigade Friday morning. Under Sheriff W. L. Ramsey organized a posse armed with rifles and shot guns and proceeded to the alleged place of rendezvous with the intention of taking the outfit in and placing them under guard until daylight, but the gallows birds had fled. After making a thorough patrol of the outskirts of the city and arranging for a night watch the citizens retired to undisturbed slumber. The city of Billings will harbor no more of this class of thugs, thieves and hobos during this year of grace, 1891.

The Billings Gazette, July 30, 1891

A SHOCKING ACCIDENT.

On the 23rd inst., Katie, an interesting little daughter of John Cannovan, aged ten years, was playing with a cap of giant powder and unwittily struck it with a stick, causing it to explode and tear her right hand into a mass of shattered bones, mangled flesh and sinewy shreds. Two of her fingers were entirely destroyed, a third badly injured, and the palm of her hand had a large hole blown through it. Dr. Leavitt was speedily summoned and endeavored to save the hand with the thumb and little finger. The accident carries with it an unusually distressing feature when it is considered that the mother has been laid away to rest in the tomb, and that this little girl is the same one who was last Summer afflicted with a broken limb, which had hardly regained its wonted strength when this second calamity befell her. Some particles of the explosive entered her breast and forehead, inflicting slight wounds. The cap had been left in the hotel by some of the miners and Mrs. Poitras placed it in her sewing machine drawer, from which the little one took it. At one time Katie had it in her mouth for quite a while. Had she shut her teeth down upon it, her head would have been blown to atoms. It is said that one of these little caps, no larger than an ordinary pistol cartridge, is charged with the strength of fifty pound powder. Miners should never leave such a dangerous agent within the reach of children.

The Atlantis (Glendale), December 28, 1879

35

—H.H. Watkins, who travels for a California tailoring establishment, showed THE GAZETTE quite a curiosity yesterday. It was a piece of tanned Indian skin. He got it, he said, from Joe Little of Stevensville, Mont., who claims to have killed the Indian from which it was taken himself. The skin is as white as snow and of about the same thickness as kid. It appears to be quite tough and would make excellent gloves. The veins in the skin, which appear to be black as ink, can be plainly seen when it is held up to the light.

The Billings Gazette Semi-Weekly, March 2, 1897

BOY KILLED BY TRAIN.

◀●▶

Otto Kimmerle Cut to Pieces by a Northern Pacific Extra Freight.

◀●▶

TRIED TO CLIMB ON CAR

◀●▶

While Train Was in Motion— No One to Blame but Himself—Coroner's Inquest.

◀●▶

The unlucky and sorrowful day, which has been looked for by trainmen and the people of Billings for some time, has come. At last the persistent efforts and carelessness of boys in attempting to climb onto moving trains has led to the death of one of them. It is indeed a costly lesson, but one that should serve as a lasting example to all other boys in Billings.

36

Otto Kimmerle, a boy about 8 years old, was run over and killed in the Northern Pacific railroad yards Tuesday evening by an extra freight train. The accident was witnessed by but one person, Arthur Ashbaugh, a boy friend, who had been in company with the Kimmerle lad. The Ashbaugh boy gave the alarm of his friend's accident to a brakeman on top of the cars, who soon stopped the train. By this time several persons had gathered around from the yards and vicinity. The injured boy was horribly mangled, the left leg being cut off close to the trunk of the body, so as to allow the entrails to protrude, the right leg was nearly severed about half way between the knee and hip, one arm was broken, his face scratched and a scalp wound inflicted on the back of the head. Still living, a stretcher was secured and the lad taken to St. Vincent's hospital, while a physician was summoned, but nothing could be done for his relief and at 7:20 the little fellow died without any apparent pain, being conscious to the last and asking several times for a drink of water.

It was about 5:15 p.m. Tuesday when an extra westbound freight train of fifty-six cars pulled into the west yards. The train had passed Twenty-ninth street and the eighth car from the last was about opposite the coal dock, when the accident occurred which cost young Kimmerle his life. The Ashbaugh boy had gone to the yard to gather up coal and was accompanied by Kimmerle. While they were there the extra freight came into the yards and as it was running slowly, the boys conceived the idea of catching on and riding. Ashbaugh, who is 11 years old, jumped on the steps of a car and rode a short distance when he jumped off. He noticed that Kimmerle was trying to get on and hollered to him not to do so, but the latter paid no heed to his friend's advice. He grabbed hold of the step with his left hand and was running along when he stubbed his toe, falling between the moving cars. Ashbaugh immediately hollered to Brakeman Milligan, who was on the rear of the train, that "there's a boy killed there." Milligan signalled to the engineer to stop and as soon as the train came to a standstill, he went back to where the boy lay. By this time several others had been attracted to the scene by Ashbaugh's cries.

Coroner Townsend called a jury Wednesday morning and held an inquest that forenoon in the court house. The witnesses examined were Al Miller, night yardmaster, E.D. Bachelor, conductor of the train, W.J. Milligan, rear brakeman and Arthur Ashbaugh. The testimony of Mr. Miller and Mr. Bachelor was of little consequence. The former was not on duty, being at his home on Montana avenue. He did not see the accident, but was there soon after it occurred. Conductor Bachelor was not on his train, having left it at the depot to register his arrival. While there he was told of the accident and went to the scene. Mr. Milligan said he was on top, about eight cars ahead of the caboose, when a boy hollered that "a boy was killed." He signalled for the train to stop. About eight cars passed before the train was brought to a standstill. Went back and saw the boy lying on the track. Injured boy asked for a drink of water. Sidetracks were clear of cars. Bell was ringing as train went through the yards.

The main witness was young Ashbaugh. He testified that both himself and Kimmerle had been to school that day. As was his usual course, Ashbaugh had gone to the Northern Pacific tracks to gather coal which had fallen from the cars. They had been accustomed to jump on to the moving trains and tried it again. The boy told a straight-forward story of how the accident happened, stating that Kimmerle had tried to jump on the train when he stubbed his toe, falling between the cars and being crushed.

This concluded the testimony and the jury then retired. It returned in a short time with a verdict to the effect that the boy had met death by being run over by a Northern Pacific freight train through his own carelessness, and completely exonerating the railroad company from all blame.

The dead boy was a son of John Kimmerle, a German stonemason, who came to Billings a year ago last spring from Missouri. He has been working lately in Carbon county and was at either Red Lodge or Gebo when the accident occurred. He is a hard working man, but has been in rather poor circumstances. His brother stonemasons and stonecutters attended to the burial services, seeing to it that the remains were properly cared for.

The Billings Gazette Semi-Weekly, September 15, 1899

BUTTE'S NIGHT OF HORROR.

Scores of People Blown Into Atoms by Mysterious Explosions.

HEROIC FIREMEN MEET THEIR DOOM.

The Darkest and Saddest Page In the History of This Commonwealth—While Surrounding a Fire Near the Montana Central Depot Many People Were Mowed Down Without a Second's Warning—More Than Forty Dead Bodies Recovered—Scenes Never Before Equalled In This Part of the World for Heartrending Affliction—Cruel Deeds of Death—It Came Like the Crack of Doom—Hundreds of Saddened Hearts— Hospitals Filled With Wounded and Dying—The Streets Crowded With Heartbroken Survivors.

BUTTE, Jan. 15.—The most terrible calamity in the history of Montana occurred this evening in this city, filling hundreds of homes with woe and placing the entire city in mourning. The extent of the awful catastrophe cannot be told to-night and the full force of the horror will not be realized for many days.

At midnight, to-night, with the awful tragedy of two hours ago appearing like a horrible dream, men and women, parents and children, husbands, relatives and friends are running from one undertaking room to another, and from one hospital to another, in the dread fear of finding some loved one who is missing.

With the fearful list of dead, the chief horror is that comparatively few have been identified and many bodies are so mutilated that they will never be recognized.

Some bodies are undoubtedly consumed in the flames, for at this hour the sickening smell of burning flesh arises from the ruins.

Called to Death.

It was at 9:55 o'clock that the quiet city was slightly stirred by an alarm of fire which called the city fire department to a little fire near the warehouses between the city proper and South Butte, not far from the Montana Central depot. The fire did not promise to be an extensive one. Probably 200 people had gathered there to watch the fire when the fire department arrived and proceeded at once to the work of extinguishing the fire.

Like the Crack of Doom.

It was 10:08 o'clock, suddenly a deafening explosion occurred, which made every building within five miles tremble and which shook the city of Butte to its foundations.

From Walkerville to South Butte and from Meaderville to Rocker a frighted people rushed from their houses, from stores, from saloons, from hotels, to see a volcano of fire extending hundreds of feet into the air.

Except to those near by there was no further horror, save the dread conjecture of what had exploded, how many might be injured in that fearful second of time and how many killed.

Windows all over Butte were shattered. Many plate glass fronts on Main street and Broadway were demolished and clear up on the Anaconda hill even the windows of the office were broken. People several blocks away from the explosion were thrown to the ground.

The Awful Horror.

If the explosion caused a dread and terror to the people miles away and safe in their homes, who shall describe the endless horrors of the scene at the explosion? How many indeed are there left to tell the awful tale?

It is believed that in the first explosion, which was the heaviest, only the firemen were killed. Spectators of the fight with the fire were thrown to the ground and temporarily. stunned, but it is not believed many, if any, citizens were killed in the first explosion.

Heroes Rushed In.

But there were heroes in the little company which had witnessed most closely the first horror, and as soon as the shock was over, while some ran in terror, others immediately began pulling the mutilated bodies of the firemen and the injured from the proximity of the flames.

From all over the city the people began moving toward the fire and the crowd had greatly increased within five minutes.

The Second Explosion.

Just about that length of time after the first explosion, a second explosion, almost equal in volume to the first, heightened the terror all over the city and spread death and desolation at the disastrous scene.

Scores Killed.

In this explosion scores of citizens were killed and injured. Parts of bodies were hurled scores of feet away.

One man near the Northern Pacific water tank was almost struck by the leg and thigh of a human being, driven by the force of dynamite from the fearful scene.

Heartrending.

There were still heroes left to help pull the shrieking wounded and groaning dying to a distance. But the people up town hesitated. There had been two explosions and there might be more. There were rumors of car loads of powder in the vicinity besides that stored in the warehouses.

Five minutes later a third explosion did come, but it was a mild one, and it is believed that very few, if any, were injured in this.

Butte's Most Awful Hour.

It had all occurred in 15 minutes, the most horrible quarter of an hour in Butte's history.

The horrible aspect of the scene, after the explosions, was beyond description. Words could give no idea of it. It presented more the appearance of a field of battle than anything else.

The dead were strewn everywhere and the cries and groans of the injured and dying presented a scene altogether unearthly.

Blood and brains were spattered all about. Here were legs and arms scattered around, and there were pieces of flesh and entrails. It was sickening.

Sickening.

Between the Northern Pacific and the Great Northern depots, a space of about 300 feet, the ground was literally covered with parts of human bodies and with the dead and injured. The scene was one of utter and absolute destruction. The houses in the vicinity were as thoroughly wrecked as if a cyclone had passed through them.

Stacks of Dead Bodies.

One of the rescuing corps gathered 27 dead bodies in one pile. Eight were in another. Two and three in other piles.

The rescuers pulled some of the bodies out still quivering, remnants of human beings still groaning, while legs and arms had been torn off. Shapeless trunks quivered and died in the arms of the living.

One man says he picked up a head with part of a shoulder attached to it just thrown at his feet and he fancied there was a dying gasp. As long as he lives he will never forget the frozen horror in the eyes of the bodyless head, made lurid by the fearful flame.

Death's Pitiless Fury.

The fire was spreading. Butte's fire department was practically annihilated. The hose cart was a wreck and the hook and ladder truck was turned on its side. The fear of more explosions kept prudent citizens from the scene of horror for a time, but the demands of humanity could not be withstood and in a very few minutes hundreds of busy, willing hands were at work.

Caring For the Dead and Injured.

Every vehicle in the city was brought into service to carry away the scores of the dead and the hundreds of injured. The hospitals were filled, the spare rooms in the hotels were taken, and private houses were thrown open where necessary.

The Anaconda Standard, January 16, 1895

AN ABORTION.—A still-born child was found on Thursday morning last, wrapped up in an old linen duster, on the ice formed over the creek in the neighborhood of the county jail. It had evidently been thrown there the night before. Probably the guilty one was too much frightened to know that the creek was frozen, and supposed the inanimate waif, prematurely robbed of existence and future life by the very one who should have fostered it, would be wafted to the rushing tide of the Missouri and be forever lost to the prurient gaze of humanity in some dark and lonely eddy in the stillness of the mountains. But such was not its fate: a kind humanizer gave it Christian burial.

The Avant Courier (Bozeman), February 22, 1872

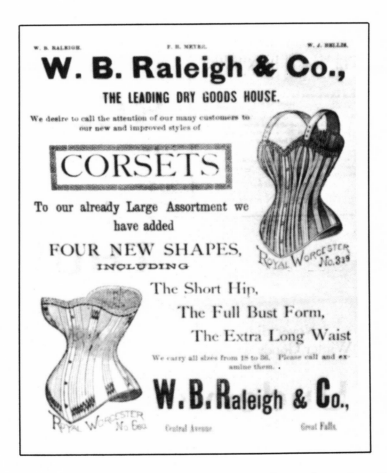

The Great Falls Leader, December 27, 1889

LADIES
"Now they defer to us a little"

WOMAN SUFFRAGE.
◄●►

Were the suffrage extended to woman is it not probable that she would go into politics with a bang and a whiz and a screech, and come out with hair parted on the side?

If women squabble and back-bite and elevate noses now over tea-table differences (as men know they do); if they call names and kick back and "scorn" opposition now in church fights (as men know they do); if they pull hair, and gnash teeth and throw plates now in family contests (as men know they do), how would they act in the political arena?

Does any sensible man suppose the male suffragist would emerge from an election not discounted, in the matter of black eyes and a broken head, by his female co-adjutor?

Wouldn't every man expect to see his wife and his daughter, opposed in sentiment, spending the month before election in disparaging the intelligence of each other's "views"—going to the polls by different roads, and returning at midnight, with hair down, and clashing tongues, to their disgrace and his misery?

Wouldn't they act over their politics as they act over their babies? And don't every man know how that is? Don't they wear you out over the watery eyes and the bullet head of the young monster? Don't they force you to "take" the nasty little thing, that spits and slobbers all over you the moment you do?

Extend the vote to woman, and every man's house would indeed soon become his castle (or his wife's). Give her the suffrage, and which, suppose you, would soon be in the ascendant, political conviction or political spite? What do you suppose each man's window glass bill would amount to per annum? Have you ever considered the appalling mortality that would accrue to back windows? Any night in the week any anxious husband might discover his Republican wife dodging about in the back-yard, shying stones at the windows of her Democratic neighbor, while, tit for tat being a female virtue, he would soon have reason to add shutters to his domicile, and fight it out with the aforesaid neighbor's husband.

Everybody remembers how Topsey set the pail of dirty water to catch the feet and spoil the finery of her enemy—extend the suffrage, and the systematic and scientific distribution of dirty water would soon be elevated into the dignity of an art. One woman wouldn't dare to pass under the windows of another woman, unless they "agreed," without an—umbrella.

No woman ever admitted the possession by any other woman of a "decent rag" to her back—every woman suspects that every other woman's hair came from the States—that all but she paint and pad and puff; put them into politics and woman's evidence would prove the entire sex a band of plug-up mess, repeaters, dough-faces and public thieves.

They claim that we withhold the suffrage because we fear them—well, we do; we fear their proverbial excess, and it is well-known that, if men avoid and detest anything, it is excess.

Now, they defer to us a little—then, they wouldn't defer at all. Now, we whirl the club—then, they would; now we monopolize the election bloody nose—then, they would share it, and any man is aware that a nose divided against itself cannot stand. Already politics and confidence in character are wide apart; but it requires a woman to blast a reputation, to spin a mile of belief from a yard of rumor, to pile up the agony against reason, to knead the preposterous into the probable, to exaggerate a yellow dog into an elephant, to make a tub stand upon any tub's bottom rather than its own. I appeal to any father of a family, but even a bachelor knows that a woman's ideas of adaptability in political affairs would bear the same practical relation to good selection of political agent, as a double-back action hen-persuader does to the egg wants of a barren fowl.

They reply that, at the worst, they would be no more culpable in politics than men; but, who makes the more noise in a fight? Who yells the louder and pulls the most hair in a mad-house? Which sex, one being wound up as tight as the other, can invent the more scandal in the same time, or meddle, or persist, or stand out against facts, or persecute for opinion's sake, the longer? Still, they demand a chance to prove or disprove their capability. Where would be the use, *we* know it would be but a waste of time, hope and effort. And if we don't know, who does?

Then, what is woman's sphere? Plainly, diaper-hemming—bread—waiting for the men to come home—resignation—quiet.

In these she shines, although it should be admitted that some men, whose opinions must not be undervalued, have questioned even here.

St. Paul (and all men must respect him) ruled women out of the churches, and men can't (so to speak) go back on St. Paul. The fact that they pay taxes counts for nothing; they should be willing to do so much for the privilege of being well governed. Again, it is claimed that many being old maids should, in the absence of protectors, have a voice in self-defence. Now, we reply that culpability only needs defence, that any old maid has voice enough, and to spare; and right or wrong, the long and short of it is, that woman shan't vote anyhow.

It is an indisputable fact, that women have no rights that men are bound to respect; and it is important to remember, that the Lords of creation have never yet fully decided against the advisability of the Hindoo mode of getting rid of bad bargains by drowning female babies, *a la* cat and puppy.

The conclusion of the matter is, that when men, sober, earnest, thoughtful men, contemplate the ocean of gab that would overwhelm politics upon the admission of women to the suffrage, they decide (and the decision is as unalterable as a Persian law, notwithstanding the weak surrender of a few old male candidates for corsets and petticoats) that this fearful thing shall not be.

J.V. BOGERT.

BOZEMAN, Feb. 17, 1872.

The Avant Courier (Bozeman), February 22, 1872

BROKEN UP—The ball at the Young America on Thursday night of last week, which bore promise, on the start, to be a splendid affair, was suddenly brought to a close, about 10 o'clock in the evening, by the ladies en masse putting on their "pretties" and suddenly decamping for their homes.—The cause of the stampede, and consequent derangement and final break-up of the party, is said to have been the surreptitious introduction into the ball room of two pretty, young milliners of town, against whom certain suspicions existed of their fair name and respectable standing in the community.

The Helena Herald, November 15, 1866

LOVE AND MURDER.

The following is a "specimen brick" from the many such soothing *billet doux* recently received by Mr. John Manning of this town: It proves that the fools are not all defunct at present writing:

MR. JNO. MANNING—*Sir:* I see you paying particular attention to one who is *too good* to *ever recognize* you more than a *dog*—you *know* that you are too *base,* too *rascally a fiend,* to *even* merit her *scorn, much less* her *smiles*—

You know that you are a *gambling, horseracing scoundrel.*

But describing your *damnable atrocities* which you know even *better* than myself is only useless, I have sworn that you never shall be more to her than you are now, leave the town within ten days or I will deprive you of that which *cannot be restored,* "I *mean* your life." I do not wish to have your blood on my hands, but one so *good,* so *pure* whose soul is *white* and *unpolluted,* must be protected from such fiends in human form as you. You have nothing to keep you—leave at once or I will send your soul to eternity.

Go, *or beware,*

PROTECTOR

We reckon the recipient of the above was not aware of his many virtues until receiving it. It will not allay the pangs of the author's unrequited affection by informing him that the "lady" in the case would not be seen walking on the same side of the street with him. 'Twas ever thus! We give notice to all concerned that we will make the "fur fly" if this disgusting nonsense is not stopped. Our citizens are sick of it.

The Missoula Pioneer, March 2, 1871

GIRLS WHO FLIRT.

While the wives and daughters of the readers of this journal have raised their voices in tones which have echoed through every portion of the Union in behalf of the suppression of the liquor traffic, and various other evils that assail the young men of today; and while they have vividly pointed out to the masculine portion of the rising generation the many vices that lie in wait for them along the highway of life, to spring up ever and anon and tempt them to digress from the paths of truth and honor, we are surprised that not one of our contributors have protested against the evils that tempt their own sex; and while they may not be so numerous, there are some of them at least, that are more deadly, if possible, than those that fall in the way of our young men. As time and space will not permit us to go into details, and we have no desire to elaborate on the subject, we shall only speak of one pernicious habit we have stood silently by and seen enlarge into a public evil. The practice of which we speak is that of flirting, and many a girl who reads this cannot realize what wrong can accrue from a little "harmless flirtation." Notwithstanding this, many a once beautiful and talented young lady, who is now eking out her existence among the haunts of sin and shame, can trace her first step from a petted child in a happy home to her entrance to the house of shame from a little "harmless flirtation." Allow us to say right here that there is no such thing as a "harmless flirtation," for danger and dishonor lurk in every crease of the silken folds of the handkerchief that is used to carry on a flirtation. Although words severe enough cannot be used in condemnation of an evil attended with such terrible consequences, and although it has wrecked lives and caused alliances in which the victim has existed a monument of a living death. And again we say, although this is true beyond a doubt, we find persons whom we would not for an instant suspect of engaging in this silly practice. Young ladies with every surrounding to make them happy, will deliberately jeopardize their happiness and good name.

We once knew a young lady of more than ordinary intellectual ability; one whom we knew to be pure in thought and action, and who stood above reproach in every other particular; yet there seemed to be a peculiar fascination attached to flirting that she could not dispel. But this mania, for we know not what else to call it, seemed to exist only in a limited degree, for she was no silly flirt, waving at every one who passed. But she was invariably seen at her window at a certain hour, waiting for a mail wagon to pass, with the driver of which she carried on a constant flirtation, extending over a period of nearly a year; but through the influence of a friend she was at last induced to give up the foolish practice entirely. Here was a young lady who numbered her friends by the score, and exactly why she suffered herself to become the party to a flirtation with a "driver," she could not explain herself: unless it seemed novel and romantic, and then we fail to see how a sensible girl could weave a romance in her imagination with the driver of a mail wagon for the hero. We give this illustration of one girl who through the timely interception of friends, came off unscathed, while hundreds of less fortunate ones have dashed on to ruin. Who has not seen a group of ladies pass and heard the question asked, "who is that blonde?" "Why, that is Miss L——, of W—— street, why do you ask?" "Oh! she is that girl who lives at No. 615, and flirts so desperately with the boys." The girl who flirts goes upon the street with the mark of Cain upon her; she is branded, and her name is taken in vain by the street loungers and echoed through the halls of business, and is even carried down into the dens of vice and by the forger and sail blower, for they all know her, formed her acquaintance through the tiny lace handkerchief she carries at her belt. We think it is safe to say no man either honors or respects a woman who will condescend to flirt with him. For when a woman becomes a flirt she compromises her character, honor and good name. She advertises her acquaintance as public property, and extends to the world a cordial invitation to grasp the accepted time and become more intimate with her charms.

Of course, it indicates that her acquaintance goes begging; or she would not seek this unfeminine-like process of enlarging her circle of friends, if such they may be called. How many a thoughtless girl, in an evil hour, has been induced to become the party to a little flirtation, just for amusement, and when too late, forever to comprehend the fact that her good name had been tainted by the breath of suspicion and dishonor; all through a little "harmless flirtation," it is then she realizes she cannot erase the stain she has made; for she is

Only a girl in this burdensome life,
Only a girl in this world of strife,
Only a girl with her good name
To pilot her over the tempting billows of shame.

The Butte City Union, February 17, 1884

HOW SOME GIRLS KISS.

The Butte girl bows her stately head,
    And fixes her stylish lips
In a firm hard way, and lets them go
    In spasmodic little snips.

The Basin girl, so gentle and sweet,
    Lets her lips meet the coming kiss
With rapturous warmth, and the youthful souls
    Float away on a sea of bliss.

The Bernice girl catches a man's moustache
    With a grip as tight as glue,
And opening a little her ruby lips,
    Pulls the kiss on like a shoe.

The Wickes girl on tiptoe stands,
    Her lips so rosy, tempting and red;
You take her cheeks in both your hands,
    Then let 'er go Murphy—Gallagher's dead.

The Comet girl—a creature divine,
    Whether wife, widow or miss—
Looks into your eyes with her star lit orbs,
    And puts her whole soul in her kiss.

The Elkhorn girl will first refuse,
    Just to have you insist and plead,
But when she finally does consent,
    Her kiss, you'll confess, takes the lead.

The Valley girl closes her dreamy eyes
    When asked to osculate,
And lets the vandal steal the kiss,
    Which she really likes first-rate.

The Helena girl says never a word,
    And you'd think she was rather tame,
With her practical view of the matter in hand,
    But she gets there just the same.

The Jefferson girl gets a grip on herself
    As she carefully takes off her hat,
And she grabs up three in a frightened way,
    Like a terrier shaking a rat.

The Corbin girl just puckers her lips,
   And in a way that's dainty and nice—
As sweet as honey, as rich as wine—
   Gives you a kiss beyond all price.

The Clancy girl neither sighs nor pines,
   Nor acts in a manner rude,
But goes about kissing in a business way,
   That catches the average dude.

The Boulder girls are neat and sweet,
   And always seem very gay;
They love to kiss, and never cheat,
   Because they're built that way.

Jefferson County Sentinel (Boulder), July 5, 1889

WHERE'S MY PAPER?

At a party held the other evening on the classic banks of the Gallatin, one of Montana's fairest daughters was present in all the pomp and panoply of the latest style of evening dress, fresh from the milliner's, Polonaise, overskirt, *ruche* trimmings and *guipure* lace to match—and was, as may naturally be supposed, the "belle of belles," the "brightest star in the galaxy." Now, this young damsel's paternal ancestor is a tiller of the soil, and had occasion to leave home for a day or two previous to the evening in question for the purpose of buying a reaper and mower, and, perhaps, also purchasing sundry yards of ribbons, etc., wherewith to bring his lovely child up to the requisite resemblance to the latest fashion plates in order to make her presentable at the sociable hop. After the fuss and flurry incident to dressing and starting for the party, the old man congratulated himself that he had the "dead sure thing" on a quiet evening wherein to regale himself with a "good, old fashioned glass of hot stuff" and the perusal of the last week's paper. But the paper was nowhere to be found; whereupon the old man grew warm; search high, search low; in cupboards and under beds; behind the bureau and out in the wood-pile was alike fruitless, until the little four-year-old hope of the family remembered that "Sal had stuffed her bustle with it." May be that old man wasn't mad, and then, again, may be he was; but, however that may be, he made a bee line for the scene of merriment, and rushing into the hall where the darling angel was tripping the "light fantastic toe," and captivating the rustic swains with the most bewitching smiles and bewildering glances, shouted with a voice like a boatswain's mate's, "Sal! where in h——l's my paper?" Ever since, a poor old man in that household bewails the poor quality of the coffee served up at his matutinal meal, and a forlorn, disconsolate maiden mourns the hardness of her fate, and vows that the coffee will not improve until that demolished pannier is replaced by a new one and she receives the newest style of hat to boot.

Bozeman Avant Courier, August 8, 1873

THE MATCHMAKER.

There are too many men in Butte leading bachelor lives who can offer no good reason for remaining in that unnatural condition. There is in this city, as there is everywhere, brave and virtuous women and girls who earn their own living, thus demonstrating their fitness for the responsibilities of life. There is in this city a good woman for every man who takes life seriously and desires to obey the natural and divine law of creation and save his immortal soul. When one looks upon the throngs that pour out of the two Catholic churches in this city and Walkerville; observes so many men who go along the streets by themselves and so many women who are without male escorts, in his heart grows up a pity for the girls and resentment for the men.

Any plan that has for its object the mingling of the sexes in rational amusement; any scheme that stimulates the social nourishment of the heart and the soul, to the end that courtship be established and marriage promoted, is of enduring benefit to religion and society. The stability of government rests upon the virtue of the citizen, and the virtue of the citizen is best conserved by the family relation. No man who is able to support a wife is doing his duty to humanity and society by living alone, and no man employed in Butte or Anaconda is without means for caring for a family.

The excuse that is frequently offered by the young man to the interrogatory, "Why don't you marry?" is something like this: "The woman I desire for wife would not have me for husband; the woman I could have I don't want." This answer is delivered in such tone of insincerity that it always prompts the second query, "Did you ever propose to the woman you like?" Invariably the reply is given: "No, it would be of no use." Of course the answer establishes his moral cowardice; either that or his desire to associate yet longer with the dissolute of the opposite sex.

Suppose, however, the young man is sincere and all that stands between him and the object of his affection is this moral cowardice (it would be altogether too charitable to call it "timidity" in this western country), what ought to be done? The day has gone by when men can carry off virgins by force and make wives of them, as the ancient founders of Troy carried off the Sabine women; and yet the world is filled with women who would not object to it. Then who will bring the youth and maiden together—the one afraid to ask and the other waiting to be asked? Nobody can do it better than the matchmaker.

The world will never realize what it owes to the match-maker. The matchmaker is perhaps unconscious of the enviable place he fills in society. There is something in his manner, or her style, which inspires confidence; which emboldens the timid to ask, "Can you do it?" sure of the reply in advance, "Why, certainly; come right along." What a moment before seemed an insurmountable obstacle van-ishes like a boulder dropped into the sea; the matchmaker has brought two people together who loved each other apart—and the young man discovers that the girl "he could not have," stood ready to be his for the asking.

Thus in the economy of life, God bestows talents upon all his creatures. Some are destined for warriors, some for statecraft, and others for matchmakers. But the greatest of these is the matchmaker, be that person man or woman. The man who speaks of the matchmaker in the breath of derision is insensible to human affection; one whose heart is a desert; who loves not children, not even a horse or a dog. The woman who scorns the matchmaker is the erstwhile coquette consumed by envy and in whose heart is the ashes of disappointment.

Tomorrow is Easter, and from that day on we expect to chronicle the social events of our people. Among them will be the affairs of the Y.M.I., whose membership is largely composed of bachelors. There are a few matchmakers in this society and the ladies' auxiliary. They are most estimable people. Their seal in a matrimonial direction will bring down blessings on their heads from the unmated.

Rocky Mountain Celt (Butte-Anaconda), April 1, 1899

—"Calamity Jane," the far-famed scout, vaquero and broncho subjugator of the western plains, came into the office of the POST last Saturday and startled the tenderfoot editor out of a year's growth. She was togged out like the ultra type of new woman in the effete east and had an air of up-to-dateiveness about her that was worth coming miles to see. Calamity used to dress entirely in masculine attire. She never could get them to fit her very well, however, and of late years has discarded the bifurcated garment for the more modest if less sensational skirt. She was en route to the National park, where she will sell her photos and biography to admirers of female emancipation during the tourist season.

The Billings Gazette Semi-Weekly, August 19, 1898

SQUAWS ON THEIR MUSCLE.

Two old-saddle-colored maidens (which their names are
not "Alvaretta" and "Minnehaha," but "Squally Jane" and
"Kootenai Mary"), of the "Lo" persuasion, had a battle-royal
here last Tuesday, in front of Haydon's stable, which was
witnessed with huge delight by a mixed crowd of some sixty
or seventy whites and Indians. Jealousy of the tender
glances bestowed upon Miss Mary by a gay deceiver who
trades in mules prompted Jane to revenge upon her rival the
slight offered to her young heart's wealth of affection by the
mule-peddler aforesaid. But she "woke up the wrong lodger."
Divesting her "lithe and graceful form" of blankets and
buffalo robes, Squally Mary "sailed" for her adversary in the
"twinkling of a bedpost." Amid a perfect whirlwind of dust
and hair, both squaws "got to work" in good earnest. A ring
was formed by the spectators, and furious betting on the
result of the encounter commenced, Kootenai Jane "wilted"
when time was called for the fifth round, and the referee
decided that Mary had "got away with the muss." As
considerable money was staked on the chances of the fight,
many appeals for "fouls" were made, but they were all
overruled by the referee. The Flathead was "handled" by
"Tapioca," and the Kootenai by "Campkettle Jack." "Bed-
rock Joe," of Bear Gulch, acted as referee. Jane's friends say
that if her "ear had been chawed" and gin administered, by
her seconds, between the rounds, they would not have lost
their money. "Chinook Sam," especially, considered himself
a much-injured innocent for allowing himself to be deceived
in the fitness of the seconds chosen to wait upon the
Kootenai Amazon.

On Saturday a female friend of the latter attacked Squally
Mary with a knife, in front of Worden's store. Some
bystanders interfered and took the weapon away from her,
leaving both damsels to fight it out with their dainty claws.
They fought for fully three-fourths of an hour, to the intense
amusement of their friends, both white and Indian. Squally
Mary received a severe cut over the right eye, but it did not
seem to "set her back" much. At length the friends of
Kootenai Jane's friend, finding she was getting the worst of

it, stopped the fight and bore their champion away, bleeding but still defiant. She said that "Squally Mary no good; all time heap fight."

The Missoula Pioneer, March 2, 1871

A WAYWARD DAUGHTER

——◄●►——

Leaves Home at Miles City and Comes to Billings with "Broncho Charlie."

——◄●►——

IN A HOUSE OF ILL FAME.

——◄●►——

Her Mother is Heart Broken— The Girl Is of Legal Age and Won't Return.

——◄●►——

Unable longer to conceal evidences of her illicit love and being determined to enter upon a life of shame, another wayward girl has broken a fond mother's heart. The latest addition to that ever increasing army of fallen women is Miss McDonald, an 18-year-old girl of Miles City, who is just now indulging in dissipation and pollution in one of the gilded palaces of sin and shame in Billings. The matter was brought to the attention of City Marshal Hubbard by W.C. Durrow of Miles City, who wrote the following letter to the Billings officer:

"I am requested to write to you in behalf of a lady here, Mrs. McDonald, whose daughter left this place Friday night, the 17th. She left here without a word of any kind. She is 18 years old, weighs about 155 pounds, has dark hair, blue eyes and was dressed in dark clothing. Her mother thinks she left here with a man who calls himself 'Broncho Charlie.' He is tall and dark complected. She bought a ticket from here to Billings. Her name is Ellen McDonald. The old lady is greatly worried over the affair and if you will interest yourself in the matter and let me know, you will have the thanks of a heart-broken mother."

Miss McDonald arrived in Billings last Saturday and is several months gone toward motherhood. She went to the Castle in the bad lands and told the mistress of the place, Mamie Lewis, that she wanted to become an inmate of the house. The Lewis woman, however, upon learning that the girl had not yet fallen so low as to enter upon a public life of shame, gave her some good advice and tried to dissuade her from her purpose. The girl, however, was determined to carry out her purpose and said that if she wasn't allowed to make her home at the Castle she would apply at one of the other houses. The mistress therefore told the girl that she might call around that night and see for herself what a life of shame was like and that if she still persisted in carrying out her purpose, after acquainting herself with the hard life led, she might try it on. Accordingly the girl returned to the Castle when the nightly orgies were at their height and plunged madly into the dissipation of the hour. She was the gayest of the gay. Such scenes were a revelation to her, and in her efforts to become proficient in her new role, she fairly outdid the other inmates. She smoked cigarettes until she was dizzy and drank whisky like an old timer. To prove to her companions that she could be as tough as the toughest, she cursed until the air was sulphurous and declared that she could put out in a single punch any two inmates of the house. She expressed her entire satisfaction with the programme and declared that the career of vice was exactly to her liking.

Last Wednesday night, Marshal Hubbard, accompanied by Chief of Police Jackson of Miles City, who was here in search of a man wanted for forgery, proceeded down the line for the purpose of ascertaining whether the girl was in town. They found her at the Castle. At the sight of the chief of police, the girl fell in a faint and when she came to acknowledged her identity. The chief tried to persuade her to accompany him back to her home at Miles City, but this she refused to do, stating that she would return alone in a few days, or just as soon as she had accumulated a little money.

As she is of legal age, she cannot be forced to go home, having passed the age of parental restraint and control. She is known in her new home as "Pumpkin Creek."

The Billings Gazette Semi-Weekly, December 24, 1897

WHISKY AND CALICO.

On Sunday evening before last a love-sick swain named Tranam—who has hitherto suffered the concealment of the tender passion to "prey upon his damaged cheek"— concluded he would "slick up a bit" and pay the object of his affection a soothing visit. The fair enslaver resides with her father at Patrick's Ferry, on Horse Prairie, and thither our hero bent his steps, gorgeous in the full effulgence of boiled shirt, freshly greased gondolas, and go-to-meeting harness. Before starting, however, he thought it expedient to hoist in about a mule's ear full of coal-oil, to get his tongue in running order for the ticklish ordeal before him. After that essential preliminary had been adjusted to his satisfaction, the pinions of impatient love quickly bore him to the domicile containing his soul's idol. But an unexpected sight awaited him when he at length found himself in the presence of his adored Gwendoline. The healthy figure of a rival named Barrett—who seemed to be having it all his own way— confronted poor Tranam, and exploded all the blissful visions he had been conjuring up since he started on his ill-timed visit. The "green-eyed lobster" instantly prompted him to the rash attempt of spreading Barrett's proboscis all over that gentleman's benign countenance. The latter, as well as his assailant, had also thrown himself outside of a compound several times that afternoon, strong enough to grow hair on his breath. The scene of sanguinary strife which followed Tranam's first blow was brought to a sudden conclusion by the girl's father kicking both warriors out of doors. The old gentleman considered such conduct as those, in presence of a lady, as highly diswrong, and he put a summary stop to it. The fight was resumed by the rivals on the wrong side of the house, and finally wound up by Tranam being reduced to a condition that will prevent his sitting up to have his bed made for six weeks to come. The latter now alleges that he wants no more Sunday night sparkin'.

A couple of spectators to the above discussion, named Buck and Davidson—also aspirants for the fair but cruel lady's favor—afterwards started in to smooth out a misunderstanding arising from the same cause that had actuated the previous skirmish. Our informant states that this encounter was so fierce that the only traces of the two men visible next morning were an old boot, two grease spots and a handful of breeches' buttons.

The Missoula Pioneer, February 23, 1871

The Post (Billings), December 16, 1882

SUNDRIES
"The true frontier ring to it"

THE BLACK HILLS "MINER."

◄●►

Some of the Typographical Tribulations of a Frontier Paper.

◄●►

The Black Hills has a newspaper already. Its title is "The Black Hills WEEKLY MINER," and its motto is "Hew to the line, let the chips fall where they may," a very good sentiment, by the way. It is a twenty column paper, edited by J.Q. Adams Brinsley, and its intelligent compositor got the forms together for the first time so that the fourth page was where the first should be, and *vice versa.* The fonts are unhappily short of "W's" and "T's," and we give some specimens to show our readers how an article looks without these essentials. The first is in reference to a proposed opposition paper to be started there, and is as follows:

"A being vvhom it vvere gross flattery to call an *idiot* talks of starting an opposition nevvspaper. VVhich of his wives will this GREEN young man bring to custer City as his vvomanaging editor, the one vvhich he used to beat at Nevvburyport, Mass., or hat one vvhom he deserted at Creston, Iovva? VVe knovv the rascal."

Not a very good opinion of his proposed contemporary, evidently. The next selection is an account of an inquest, or rather a proposed one, and is very good:

"Montana Jim, who lives up in Coyote street, vvas found on tuesday last apparently dead and a bottle of vvhisky in his hand, vvhich gave rise to the hypothesis of congestion of the brain. Over the remains vvhat can only be styled an unseemly dispute took place as to vvho should hold the inquest, Judge thomas, sheriff, holding that he vvas qualified by virtue of the vox populi of his election, vvhile Major Bloker claimed the privilege as a territorial official, the dispute being finally left to the arbitrament of euchre. Chairs and tables being somevvhat scarce, Montana Jim's alleged corpse vvas utilized in the latter capacity under vvhich arrangement the game progressed satisfactorily till with the game 6 and 6 (7 points being played) and each player tvvo tricks in, Judge thomas played the ace of trumps, the right having been played and the left, as he thought, at the bottom of the pack, vvhen Major Bloker put down the left bovver vvith a triumphant blovv of his fist on the table, being the corpse of Montana Jim, vvho being suddenly avvakened from his trance, arose and pitched into the Major, nor could he for some time be pacified."

This has the true frontier ring to it, and reminds one of some of Twain's anecdotes. The MINER is a currency reform paper and says on that subject:

"VVe vvish emphatically to make knovvn our position with regard to the currency question. VVe are opposed to the kings of VVall street, vvho grind the honest farmer to the vvall. VVe vvill be for vvorthy VVilliam Allen, of Ohio, first, last and all the vvhile."

Butte Miner, June 3, 1876

WEATHER SIGNALS.

Explanations of the Flags
Displayed on the Shoemaker Building.

The Farmers' club has erected a staff on the Shoemaker building and the signals are now displayed daily by Local Observer Dr. E.P. Townsend. They are received from Helena daily at 10 a.m. and the forecast is for the ensuing twenty-four hours. The forecast for Friday is local snow, decidedly colder tonight, fair Saturday. Below is an explanation of the signals:

White flag alone indicates fair weather with stationary temperature.

Blue flag alone, rain or snow with stationary temperature.

White and blue flag alone, local rain with stationary temperature.

White flag with triangular flag above, fair weather and warmer.

White flag with triangular flag below, fair weather and colder.

Blue flag with triangular flag above, warmer weather with rain or snow.

Blue flag with triangular flag below, colder weather with rain or snow.

Blue and white flag with triangular flag above, warmer weather with local rains.

Blue and white flag with triangular flag below, colder weather with local rains.

White flag with white flag below with black center, cold wave.

Blue flag with white flag below with black center, wet weather, cold wave.

The Billings Gazette, April 6, 1895

WARM RECEPTION.

The Times Called On
By Distinguished and Promiscuous Visitors.

◄●►

In order to acquaint our distant readers with all the facts it is necessary to go back to the morning of Friday, Oct. 23, when Mrs. Plume claims a burglar entered her residence (her husband does not reside in town) whereupon she took her revolver and with heroic courage drove him through the window, firing several shots and following him into the streets. She claimed to have been shot at by the burglar, the ball passing through her nightdress and just grazing her flesh. Several men were almost instantly on the scene and a corn patch where the robber was supposed to be concealed was surrounded and guarded until morning. But no burglar nor evidence of one was found, and it was generally concluded that the whole affair was a hoax, that there was no burglar there at all, and that Mrs. Plume was seeking notoriety and a reputation for unusual daring. After carefully looking into the facts and allegations such was our emphatic belief. It was the duty of the TIMES to make some kind of a report of the affair, as our subscribers pay for the news and have a right to expect it. With no desire to be harsh, on the contrary to be as mild and lenient as possible, the affair was presented in our last issue under the heading, "A New Fangled Ghost." In that report Mrs. Plume's name was not mentioned, neither was her residence, nor would readers outside of Missoula know who was referred to. Not less could have been said with any regard for the circumstances, and had we said more it would certainly have been worse. But Mrs. Plume and one C.F. Hawks, proprietor of an alleged livery stable on Front street, who occupies a room at the Plume residence, took great offence at the article. Said Hawks particularly pranced about like a wild Senegambian and used invectives that would have made the author of all that is vile and filthy hide his head in shame.

The outcome was a thrilling scene in this office Saturday

afternoon. A stranger came in and stood by the stove, and in a couple of minutes in came the irate Mrs. Plume, who, as quick as a flash, raised a rawhide and struck a poorly directed blow at the TIMES' pen-pusher. She was instantly caught by the arms, but the stranger, who was her confederate, grabbed the editor around the body, it having evidently been arranged that he would hold the TIMES' Goliath while she would administer a sound threshing as our punishment for trying to tell the truth. At this juncture the aforesaid Hawks came cowardly in at the rear door and took part in the affray as an assistant and right-hand bower. The TIMES' printers—Le Roy and Jones—were already on hand and exhibited a strength that would have astonished the powerful Hercules in Robinson's circus. The affair was short and to the point, and the three invaders who sought to paralyze the TIMES were tumbled into the street. It was a complete fizzle, yet had it been advertised it would have had a crowded audience. The venerable Printer Jones lost his spectacles and Le Roy suffered a sprained thumb, which was the extent of the damage, and the cowhiders went away as curs would naturally go that had been struck with a whip.

The three parties—C.F. Hawks, Mrs. Plume and W.J. Plume—were arrested on a charge of assault and battery and each fined $10 and costs, amounting to $24.90 in each case, in Justice Sloane's court Monday.

Missoula County Times, November 4, 1885

"A DEVIL OF A TIME!"

What have we as people of Butte done to excite the ire of old father Time that he has never yet seen fit to give us a uniform rate by which to regulate our goings out and comings in? It can't be that he regards us of not sufficient importance to be worthy of notice, for Deer Lodge, Missoula and other places numbering not more than half our population can all get up and go to bed at the same hour if they are so inclined. But here in Butte, one man breakfasts at seven by candle-light and another at seven by broad daylight, and all because one man has Deer Lodge time and another Helena, and a third that of California. Each mill runs on its own time, and there is at least an hour's variation in their different calculations. If a meeting is appointed for eight o'clock, one man after another lags in, quite well satisfied that he has observed the appointed hour to the minute, judging by his chronometer, until the hour has slipped by and left the first comers who are also on time by their watches all out of patience. If one of our surveyors or some one else does not come to the rescue, we will have to adopt Captain Cuttle's plan, which he said was a very good one, to turn our watches forward a quarter of an hour in the morning and back half an hour at night, and thus come somewhere near having the same time as our neighbors. Joking aside, it is clearly the duty of some one to take the matter of time in hand and not have denizens of Butte obliged daily to hear it said that "Butte time is a Devil of a time." Will not our resident surveyor deign to make a note of this and take an observation for the benefit of the public?

Butte Miner, February 6, 1877

—News reaches Billings of a shooting scrape last Monday night near Hutton post office, Custer county. A meeting was being held in the schoolhouse in that district to discuss the advisability of petitioning the commissioners for a jail and a peace officer, a practical demonstration for the necessity of which was furnished by a free fight. During the melee Frank Ingram was shot in the leg by C.A. Wasson, the chairman of the meeting. The injured man was taken to Fort Custer for treatment and Wasson was taken to Miles City by Sheriff Gibbs.

The Billings Gazette Semi-Weekly, March 5, 1897

TOUGH ON THE PASSENGERS.

Stories of Frightful Suffering Come from Garrison.

From all accounts received it appears that a large number of travelers suffered great hardships at Garrison Junction on last Friday night, Saturday and Saturday night. The Utah Northern train conveying 200 passengers destined for points along the Northern Pacific, reached Garrison Friday night a half hour after the Northern Pacific train had passed. The passengers crowded into the depot, which was entirely inadequate to accommodate so many or even afford standing room. There were only two small benches in the depot, yet among the passengers were quite a number of ladies having babies in their arms and small children to take care of. In this situation they were compelled to wait from Friday night until 2 o'clock Sunday morning. A part of the women were compelled to stand while the rest occupied the seats, and in the crowd and confusion there was neither sleep nor rest for any one. The men stood until, overcome by exhaustion, they sank down, one by one, on the floor swimming deep with melted snow, dirt and tobacco juice. It was a frightful experience in which all suffered equally. Finally some of the men asked leave to get into a caboose which was out on a side-track, but were refused, we are informed, when they proceeded to the car and burst in the door. The women standing in the depot then endeavored to get in the car, but before they could reach it, it was filled with men, and they could only retrace their steps. Many of the passengers were worn out when they reached the junction, having come a long distance, and their suffering during those many hours must have been intense. The Northern Pacific train arrived at 2 A.M. on Sunday, but that was crowded and many were still compelled to stand. Quite a number got off the train here and sought rest in our hotels.

Missoula County Times, February 20, 1884

69

BLOODY SLUGGERS.

―◄●►―

Two-Ounce Gloves Draw Much Claret from Two Heavy-Weights—Incidents.

―◄●►―

There is something in contests of endurance, whether between men or animals, so fascinating to the average man with good red blood in his veins that he will quietly leave a warm wife abed at 3 o'clock in the morning, risk a large percentage of his income in making bets, and endure other equally trying hardships to witness one. The same early-risers are upholders of the law, and would be the first to stop a runaway team, volunteer to quell an Indian outbreak, or shoulder a musket if their country's honor was endangered. But they would also be the first to leave the desk or work-bench to look at a dog fight or a rough-and-tumble scrap, or be on-lookers at a contest, in which the principals are eager to bust the heads of each other for local fame and a little silver, or to gratify personal hatred.

From the day that Bill McGeehan and Con Morris had the go-as-they-pleased scrap at the corner of First-avenue South and Second street there has been more or less pugilistic oratory as to which was the better man. The Morris partisans claiming that Con was the younger, could stand more punishment, had better wind, and could

Down the "Old Man"

in a fight to a finish; while McGeehan's friends swore that Bill was the more scienced, the hardest hitter, and could knock out the "big duffer" in the first round. Finally, articles were agreed to and a forfeit deposited. The principals began training and the fight was announced for the morning of the 5th. Several good citizens at once took steps to prevent the meeting; even threatening the arrest of all prominent citizens who took any part in aiding or abetting the fight.

The morning of the 5th came and went, and the match was said to be off. Morris continued at work plastering; while McGeehan spent the time in

Studying the Currents

of the mighty Missouri, so as to have the best of it in his boat race with Dan McKay. Thus were the fears of the g. c.'s allayed; and they continued the study of the law, the barter and sale of real estate, and the building of houses of worship. But the p. c.'s were going to have their fun all the same. Sunday a quiet tip was given to the boys, and by the time the last religious service was concluded every man, woman and child in Great Falls knew that the delayed fight was to come off, for sure, early Monday morning. So much for a quiet tip. One q. t. was that Giant Spring park was to be the scene of Morris' defeat; another, that McGeehan was to be downed at the slaughter house on the Johnstown side of the river. But the insiders were

Better Posted,

and at 2 o'clock this morning boats, with muffled oars, began to shove off silently from the docks of Capt. Taylor and Dunlap & Mitchell, headed up stream; while the rattling rumble of heavily-laden wagons aroused the quiet people of First-avenue South from untroubled sleep, and broke up several all-night five-cent stud games then going on in the saloons located on that thoroughfare. The wagons headed for Dexter's ferry, where they crossed the river, took the road that leads through deserted Johnstown and pulled up at the Sun river ferry landing. Here a halt had to be made, as the ferryman had not anticipated so large a volume of business so early in the morning and was asleep. Finally the raging Sun was crossed, and a small crowd who had arrived by boats could be seen down near the river bank by the railroad grade. At that hour—3 o'clock—probably thirty p. c.'s and two of the girls were on the ground. The crowd gradually grew until, at 5 o'clock, about 100 people were present.

The ring was pitched and the principals on the ground, McGeehan being the first to shie his hat inside the charmed square circle. McGeehan stripped to the buff, wearing white trunks and drawers. His colors were crimson red. Morris fought the fight in white drawers and undershirt, and dark green colors. The rules (POLICE GAZETTE) governing the fight and articles of agreement were then read, time-keepers appointed, a referee chosen and the seconds tossed up for choice of corners. McGeehan's second won the toss and selected the southeast corner. Time was called, and both men toed the scratch, shook hands and the fight commenced at 5:06 o'clock.

Round One.—After a little cautious sparring by both parties, McGeehan got in a right-hander on Morris' left cheek, drawing first blood, and in return got two or three body blows. They fought all around the ring and did good work.

Round Two.—The second round opened as did the first. McGeehan dodged a swinging left-hand upper cut, but caught a body blow that brought him to his knees. On regaining his feet he landed one on Morris' neck that seemed to anger the plasterer, and the remainder of the round was a slugging contest, Morris fighting McGeehan into the southeast corner and against the ropes. As the time-keepers yelled "Time," McGeehan's second yelled "Foul." The claim was not allowed. Morris had the best of the round.

Round Three.—At the beginning both began to show signs of punishment on the face, and blood was flowing freely. Morris forced the fighting; but the "old man" was active and skillfully dodged several vicious left-handers. Finally Morris landed one square on McGeehan's mouth which knocked him clear off his feet. First knock-down for Morris. In this round claims of "foul" and "time's up" were made by both parties. But the referee said the men had to fight on their merits, and that no technical claims of foul would be allowed.

Round Four.—The fighting in this round was terrific, both parties giving and taking punishment. Morris got in an under-cut on McGeehan's right jaw, and got three stingers in the left side of his neck in return. The round ended with Morris apparently the fresher of the two, and bets were freely offered that he would win the fight.

Round Five.—This was one of the hardest contested rounds of the thirteen, and was a two-hander from start to finish. Morris fought McGeehan to his corner,and gave the "old man" severe punishment. They clinched and the referee yelled "break away," but before doing so Morris tripped McGeehan and the latter fell in the middle of the ring as time was called. This raised another claim of foul, as under the rules no wrestling is allowed. But the referee emphatically said, "No!" Up to the close of this round Morris had the best of it, but he claims to have broken his left hand in the fourth round when he had McGeehan in his corner, and for the remainder of the fight was handicapped.

Round Six.—In this round McGeehan got his second clean knock-down, which didn't seem to hurt him; but the round ended to Morris' advantage.

Round Seven.—Neither received much punishment.

Round Eight.—Both men came up smiling but weak, and after each passage would clinch and be ordered to break away. At the seventh or eighth hug Morris tripped McGeehan, and the latter's friends again claimed a foul, alleging that the rules barred wrestling. The referee decided that both men were so weak that one or the other had to fall as they came together. Time called. The time-keepers began to review the referee's decisions and make comments on the staying qualities of their favorites, and before they found out that a time-keeper should be as dumb as an oyster, a minute and twenty-eight seconds had elapsed. They both yelled at the same time and the ninth round commenced.

McGeehan Gets His Second Wind.

Round Nine.—The extra seconds rest had a good effect, and both men appeared fresh. McGeehan led and got in two good ones on Morris' neck, which seemed to daze the latter, and from that time to the close of the fight he apparently had the advantage. His friends yelled themselves hoarse in giving him pointers, and made the referee's position one not to be envied.

The tenth, eleventh and twelfth rounds were a repetition of the ninth. McGeehan landing his right on Morris' neck and ribs, aiming apparently to do him up by hitting him repeatedly on the same spot; but Morris stood the punishment, and occasionally got in a blow that staggered his opponent. In the tenth round McGeehan knocked Morris down, but failed to follow up the advantage.

Round Thirteen.—This round commenced amid an uproar of yells by the partisans of the two men. The referee tried hard to maintain order, without success. Several blows were exchanged, but both were pretty well played out. In fact they clinched so often that the referee was the only man who was doing any work. He had to forcibly make them break away so often that he wisely concluded that the men had received enough punishment and "a draw" the proper decision to make at the time. At first this was opposed by the crowd and seconds, but the referee was firm and finally his decision was accepted by all parties as a just and proper one.

McGeehan then walked over to Morris' corner and shook the latter by the hand, saying, "Con, you are a good one and game man." Morris replied, "Bill, you are a clever old man," and the

Fight Was Over

at 6:12. Both men were pretty badly punished about the face, McGeehan being the worst disfigured of the two, both eyes being nearly closed, three teeth gone and cuts on the head that required seven stitches to hold together. Morris had one bad eye, and the left side of his neck was greatly enlarged. Both immediately returned with friends to town. McGeehan is the fairest fighter of the two, and the more scientific, but Morris has age in his favor and the nerve to stand much punishment. Neither are two-handed fighters, Morris seldom using his right, or McGeehan his left.

The gate receipts—over $250—were evenly divided between the two men, which will keep them in spending money until they are able to resume their legitimate vocations.

The 100 prominent citizens and the 2 girls returned to town in time for breakfast and business, and by 8 o'clock not a man could be found who witnessed the fight. However, a full list of those present will be printed for private distribution, so their names can be handed down to posterity as law-abiding citizens of a God-fearing community.

Great Falls Tribune Semi Weekly, July 13, 1887

—"Crow" Davis has been in town this week and claims that on the morning of the 5th, the Sioux Indians who furnished amusement for the crowds at Fort Custer the Fourth, were issued a wagon load of dogs as rations.

The Billings Gazette, July 13, 1895

—No less than fourteen dog fights have occurred in front of the palatial Broadwater-Pepin Co. establishment since the last issue of the EAGLE. Last Monday afternoon a dozen or more contentious brutes engaged in a controversy over the possession of favors of the canine belle of the city. While the battle was raging furiously an insignificant little yellow phist eloped with the canine belle. And now, we suppose, the other pups are wondering what they were fighting for. The EAGLE'S horse editor is compelled to notice these trifling incidents in order to save his princely salary from the sharp edge of the heavy editor's pruning knife. No, thanks, Mr. Broadwater; no more Budweiser today.

The Milk River Eagle (Havre), September 23, 1898

A WOLF IN SHEEP'S CLOTHING.

◀●▶

Geo. Mitchell, A Mouthy Nondescript

◀●▶

Fired Out of the Republican Convention By Wrathy Colored Delegates.

◀●▶

George Mitchell is a colored man, mouthy, conceited, presumptious and suffering with a virulent case of swell head. He is a political acrobat of the worst type. He came to this city a few months ago and settled in the first ward. He has done odd jobs until the campaign opened. George is a slick looking fellow with a Websterian head as smooth as a billiard ball and with a pair of poodle dog eyes and large ears on either side. At first glance he would be taken for a Louisiana preacher or ballot box stuffer. His suavity of manner and soft talk are captivating, hence George soon ingratiated himself into the confidence of the simple plain folks of the First ward and as he carries in his side pockets a collection of almanacs, stale congressional records and the like he soon was looked upon as the coming man of his ward. George is very loquacious and long-winded and it is no uncommon thing for him to spellbind the eager and attentive First warders for hours at the time. By and by the ward primaries came on and George waxed happy as in the days of yore down in sweet Iberville where the sugar cane grows. He marshaled his club together in a shack with beer kegs for seats and a kerosene barrel for a rostrum and told his men that now was the opportunity of their lives and that they must stand by him for delegate to the Republican county convention. On the night of the primaries the said George at the head of his club marched in and took possession of the First ward, electing himself and eleven white men as delegates to the county convention. This is the way George Mitchell got into our republican county convention. No sooner was the convention called to order than George was on his feet and from that time on so obtrusive, obstreperous and obnoxious did he become that the whole convention as with one accord ordered him to dry up and sit down. But George lacks modesty as well as good sense and with his ears flapping he persisted in braying and sawing the air with meaningless motions. It was at this juncture that the colored delegates and spectators ceased to forbear and their pent up indignation asserted itself in a spontaneous outbreak of just retribution and as the deadly cyclone swooped they down upon the unsuspecting blatherskite. They laid hands on his brawny form and told him he must go, as he had disgraced his people quite long enough. George bucked, but in the eyes of these determined men he saw pent up vengeance, so he quietly allowed himself to be thrust bodily out of the convention hall. Thus ended one of the most embarrassing episodes it has ever been our misfortune to chronicle. The colored delegates to our conventions have uniformly been men of standing in the community and who have reflected credit upon us as a people, hence a feeling of mortification exists over this unfortunate occurrence. Better that the 1st send no colored delegate in the future if the men thereof are so gullible as to allow any tramp, who may gather about

76

himself a following, to thrust himself forward as the representative of the colored people of that ward, of whom there are many and eminently respectable ones at that. It behooves the leaders of the First to look to their reputation in the future and shut out men who go about snorting and braying and posing as representative colored men. Representative colored men are not built that way. Give us straight goods hereafter or none at all. The colored citizens of this city will never again tolerate a man like Mitchell to be palmed off by the First or any other ward as a selected representative of their race.

The Colored Citizen (Helena), September 10, 1894

TIMES' CORRESPONDENCE.

BOULDER VALLEY, M.T.
April 15, 1870.

MR. EDITOR: As usual, "all's well;" labor, the progenitor of all blessings, manifests itself in every quarter, and judging from the "sowing" prognostic of great reaping, a golden harvest will dawn upon us in proper time and season, without fail. Saturday the 23rd inst., is representing day on Spring Bar. Let all those absent ones interested smell a "big mice" and attend.

The price of beef cattle is very high, though by no means scarce; horseflesh too is in brisk demand. I do not exactly know the quotations, as it is usually bought and sold by the bulk or on foot, but as already remarked, at pretty high figures. Boulder abounds in race nags, but money is tight and easy on the "score."

Yesterday, for the first time in a coon's age I had vacation to visit Jefferson valley, things there I observed, looked as of yore, especially the old Milk ranch. A marked increase in stock did, however, not escape my notice, and many "mikles make a muckle" is a sober adage, truly illustrated in life size, by industrious stock-raisers, who generally keep an eye on the market. Mine host at the celebrated "White Hall" bade me welcome, and under his kind and paternal care I felt "as snug as a bug in a rug."

In the morning I was suddenly surprised at the sight of the Chinese emigration advance guard. There was food for my curiosity. I sat and watched their movements until my stomach turned at their filthy habits. Maj. Brooke, my "host" aforesaid, perceiving my ghastly countenance, proposed forthy drops of Rocky Mountain dew, to be taken "inwardly." Now, myself and the Major differ strongly in politics, but I second the motion, and with the aid of Gov. Pollenger and Kirkendall, men who know how to measure hay in the cock or stock, the proposition was adopted and put in immediate effect.

A Close Call.

What opinion and sympathy I hitherto entertained for the Celestial crew was here reduced to "0." There they were, the bucks in the Hotel, washing, gorging, spitting and coughing, using towels for pocket handkerchiefs, more nimble than graceful, while their women were kept out like so many dogs, crawling around the coach to protect themselves against a bitter cold and piercing wind. When I learned that such treatment to their women is a part of their religion, I became again fatally ill at heart and all that kept me from fainting away was an additional forthy drops and a fraction over.

At last the driver's merry voice sounded in my ears, all aboard for Boulder.—I rushed, but alas, only in time to find the coach filled up to the guards with these almond eyed heathens. There was no alternative left. I had either to allow myself to be strapped on the boot with the luggage, or ride home on foot. I preferred the former and away we sailed, but I could not become reconciled to my cruel situation, but at every jolt I vexed and swelled up with indignation until the strap bursted, and by some remarkable bounce I struck a tremendous summersault over the front of the coach, driver and all, and landed under the tongue. The nigh wheeler informed me of that fact by dashing out my brains, rough shod, then the hind wheels ran simultaneously over the back of my neck and severed the jugular vein both above and below the nipple. I laid there speechless, while life was ebbing away, cursing Mongolians like a Rhinelander, but my sorrow had not yet reached its climax, the worst of all became only known to me after the first calamity was all over. "I broke the crystal of my watch and lost my pipe stem." It's hard, but must be endured. On my arrival home I was arrested for an unsuccessful attempt at suicide and will be hung on the 23rd inst., at 10 o'clock a.m. if the weather will permit. So adieu, remember

GALLON.

The Montana Capital Times (Virginia City), April 23, 1870

—A Chinaman came in on the coach this morning bound for Benton and thoughtlessly stepped off the vehicle when near the post-office. Some one of the bystanders standing hard by, called out: "Come on boys, here's a China." The almond-eyed son of the Flowery Kingdom took the cue on the instant, and jumped fully three feet perpendicular in the air, and as soon as he struck the sidewalk, made a rush for the coach in a manner which would delight the heart of the most radical Chinese exterminator.

Great Falls Tribune Semi Weekly, July 30, 1887

FROM THE FRONT.

◄●►

Our readers might have read a notice, about the 1st of July, of the departure of two gentlemen by the name of John W. Brown and George W. Rea, who intended prospecting the head sources of Snake and Wind river, both of which raise in the same range. They returned yesterday, looking rough but hearty, and having the pedal extremities encased in elk skin shoes, which are cut from the knee joint of that animal, forming a perfect moccasin, which is drawn over the feet while green and suffered to dry, thus making a covering tight almost as the skin itself. They are available for the purpose of wear, but are somewhat difficult to remove, requiring the application of cold steel to make them yield their rather novel purposes. These two hardy adventurers performed a journey deemed hazardous in the extreme by all mountain men. After leaving this city, they met but few white men. When on the eastern slope of the Wind River Mountains, about three hundred miles from here, on the 17th of July, they were attacked by a band of fifteen Sioux, and after a severe engagement, in which the boys succeeded in a final treaty of peace with five of the varmints. The rest, not deeming the "medicine talk" of our heroes very healthy, *abequatulated.* Rea's horse was shot in two places. It is their intention to return immediately, as they are fully convinced good placer and quartz diggings exist in that range. They report game of all descriptions as exceedingly abundant, and the scenery of the country as most charming.

If Government really desires peace with these "noble red men," let her drop peace commissioners and bureau military chieftans; appropriate two million dollars annually for a few years to defray expenses; let the balance of the task to the hardy mountaineer, and we venture nothing in saying that peace will be established, as enduring as the mountains which compose the Wind River Range.

Montana Democrat Tri-Weekly (Virginia City), August 8, 1868

—Two Flathead men are going into the elk raising business and already have eight of the animals partially domesticated. They were hunted on snow shoes and captured with a lariat.

The Billings Gazette, April 13, 1895

A GREY HAIRED HERMIT.

◄●►

Trapper Tulley Subsists on
Flour, Sugar and Martin Meat For

◄●►

Five Months in the Mountains
Without Seeing a Living Person.

◄●►

A few days since E.H. Cooper and George Chilson returned from their ten days trip to the coal banks. Their menu most of the time consisted of flour and water. After leaving the valley they had to travel on snow shoes, and only took enough provisions for one day expecting to get plenty of flour, bacon, salt and pepper from their cache along the trail, but on reaching the spot they found the snow so deep and hard that it was impossible to get them, and were obliged to go on to their cabin without refreshing the inner man. When near the coal camp they met a specimen that rather startled even their sturdy nerves. The object which confronted them had long grey bushy hair and beard, no part of the face being visible. His first exclamation on discovering the intruders was, "by G—d! there's some white men." The personage before them proved to be an old trapper named Tulley, who had wandered into their cabin, and being snow bound, had taken possession of it and the provisions stored therein. He had not seen a white person for over five months, and had had nothing to eat except flour and sugar—no salt, pepper nor baking powder. Cooper and Chilson had about three tons of hay put up for spring, but the old hermit had turned his horse loose in the hay corrall and after the hay was gone the cayuse passed in his immortal checks. The old man was asked how he had enjoyed his winter's resort and replied "first-rate," but it would have been more pleasant if he had had his gun, which for some reason he had left by a tree along the trail where it was found by the boys on their way to the cabin. He said he had tried to kill deer and moose

81

with his snow shoe pole by running them into deep snow and striking them on the back but could not bring them down as the moose were too lively for the old man who is over sixty years of age. He caught three martin while the boys were there and cooked and ate them without pepper or salt. Cooper said he was invited to dine, but as his stomach was not in martin-eating order he was obliged to decline the proffered hospitality. Upon departing the boys gave him the combination to their cache, and told him to help himself as they had plenty and would never see a man suffer as long as they had anything to donate.

The Inter-Lake (Demersville), April 11, 1890

FISTIANA.

"HEAVY" AND "LIGHT" WEIGHTS.

A fight occurred on the corner of Bridge street, yesterday, between a man about seventy-five years of age, and a boy of some fourteen summers. It came about in this wise: The boy sitting on a wood-pile, wearing a pair of moccasins; the old man coming down street, addresses him thus: "Halloa, young man, what tribe do you belong to? The Blackfeet or Flatheads?" Boy: "I don't know, sir, that it is any of your business." Old man: "Look here, sonny, I am seventy-five years old; but notwithstanding all that, I can whip h——l out of you in just five minutes!" The boy, thinking the old gentleman a little hasty in his conclusion, replied: "I don't care if you are seventy-five years old, you can't whip me in twenty-five minutes." The old man, proposing to make his word good, let go with his "right duke" and brought him to mother earth, and claimed the first knock down. The boy came to time beautifully, clinched his ancient antagonist, and both went to the ground together, the latter occupying the second best position. The boy, profiting by the advantage gained, put the old gent's eyes in mourning, which will probably last him for several days. "First blood" claimed for the juvenile, which was allowed by the friends of his opponent. The by-standers did not interfere in any way, thinking it about "six of one, a half dozen of the other." The boy was declared the victor on the fifth or sixth round, but seemed to feel very much mortified to think that necessity had compelled him to have an altercation with one who was so much his senior in years.

Helena Weekly Herald, June 4, 1886

A SCAMP AND A RASCAL—A fellow named Alexander N. Burczynski, who has resided in this vicinity for several years past, and followed the vocation of sheep herder and freighter, skipped over into Canada last week, leaving a number of disconsolate creditors to mourn the loss of several hundreds of dollars, which they had trusted him to in order to help him along. Burczynski is as cold blooded as a snake and possesses the principle of an alligator, he would beat his mother or his best friend he had. He is by birth a Polander, but is a naturalized citizen, thief, liar, scoundrel, scamp and reprobate of America. In appearance he looks like a horse thief, and would pass for one in any civilized country. He is about 5 feet 6 inches in height, dark complexioned, black eyes, hair and moustache, very white teeth, which he shows to advantage when he grins, which is almost continually. Is an inveterate cigarette sucker, and will play 15-ball all day if he can find as big a fool as himself to play with him.

Great Falls Tribune, August 21, 1886

Anaconda Weekly Review, August 1, 1889

84

INDEX

Additional copies of *Browsing in the Morgue* are available at Montana bookstores or for $4.95 each from Barlow Press, P.O. Box 5403, Helena, Montana 59604.

Other Barlow Press publications include The Constitution of the United States of America and a reprint of *The Weekly Montana Republican's* delightful 1869 Virginia City serial, *A Yellowstone Expedition*. Both volumes were composed in hand-set type, printed by hand on a 1927 Chandler & Price platen press, and bound in softcover by hand. We welcome submissions of original fiction, poetry, essays, profiles, and journals; suggestions for historical reprints; and orders for fine hand-set, hand-printed job work such as invitations, greeting or business cards, stationery, brochures, posters, and broadsides.